EASY MONEY

EASY MONEY

Philip Coggan

P

PROFILE BOOKS

First published in Great Britain in 2001 by
Profile Books Ltd
58A Hatton Garden
London ECIN 8LX
www.profilebooks.co.uk

10 9 8 7 6 5 4 3 2 1

Typeset in Minion by MacGuru
info@macguru.org.uk

Printed and bound in Great Britain by
Clays, Bungay, Suffolk

A CIP catalogue record for this book is available from the British Library.

ISBN 1 86197 275 x

To Sandie

Contents

Acknowledgements

First, and definitely most, I would like to thank my wife, Sandie. Not only has she been unfailingly supportive through the long hours of writing the book but she has been a constant source of ideas and contacts. The book could not have been written without her.

Secondly, I would like to thank my colleagues at the *Financial Times*. Working at the *FT* is a privilege, because of the adult way in which it treats its employees and because of the professionalism and knowledge of its staff. Particular thanks are due to Thorold Barker, Caroline Daniel, Chris Dunkley, James Mackintosh and Astrid Wendlandt. But the articles of Paul Abrahams, Richard Tomkins and Richard Waters have also been immensely helpful. And I would also like to thank Richard Lambert, the editor, and John Ridding, the managing editor, for allowing me to pursue this project.

Inevitably, some of this book is based on ideas I have already expressed in *FT* articles or in my column of FT.com. The vast bulk of quotations in this book are taken from interviews or e-mails conducted by the author specifically for the book. I have indicated the exceptions, including a few quotes that I garnered in the course of articles for the newspaper.

Thanks are accordingly due to all the interviewees – Ajaz Ahmed, Jonathan Ainsley, Victor Basta, Paul Bellringer, Martin Belsham, David Bowen, David Buik, Tim Carey, Andy Clifton, John Delaney, Mark Eccleston, Lewis Findlay, Rob Golding, Ross Greenwood, Debs Harris, Tony Hobman, Richard Hunter, Jeremy King, Paul Lubbock, Lucy Marcus, Angus McCrone, Mick McLoughlin, Robert Norton, Chris Price, Gerda

Reith, Nigel Reynolds, Sarab Singh, Justin Urquhart Stewart and Stuart Wheeler.

Thanks also to the readers who e-mailed me with their views: Steve Bennetts, Liz Cameron, Joe Cittern, Malwa Cotton, Billy Fitzgerald, Simon Gordon, Robert Griffiths, James McCarthy, Martin Newton, Lorenz Nwachuku, Stephen Rivett and Peter Wilson.

I am also grateful to the many analysts and economists whom I speak to on a regular basis at the *FT*. While, as a group, they tend to be over-optimistic about individual stocks, their economic and industrial work is of an extremely high standard. I have referred to some of their reports within the book and given full citations where possible.

Any book covering the stock market and the internet is bound to be a little out-of-date by the time it appears. I am writing this in December 2000 for a planned publication date in June 2001. Perhaps all the dotcom stocks will have rebounded by then. Even if they have, I believe the main structural points of this book will still be correct.

Finally, I would like to thank my publisher Andrew Franklin of Profile Books, who has shown faith in me to write a book for the second time, after a gap of fifteen years. I hope this effort makes him some easy money.

Introduction

What were the chances of someone like me
netting £1m within 12 months?

Internet employee

When my shares were in profit, it was too easy, it was like money for free.

Private investor

They don't see it as investment, they see it as a game.

Stockbroker

I have a friend in Yorkshire – a pig farmer – who was trading shares.
The Ferrari brochure arrived on his mat the day the market collapsed.

Day trader

We would all, save for the odd monk or diehard socialist, like to have more money. Indeed, most of us will have fantasised about having millions at some point or other.

But for much of our lives, it has seemed out of the question. Inherit it? Alas, Dad was a teacher or a bus conductor. Earn it? That probably involves thirty years of eighteen-hour days that are likely to end in a heart attack or a rude letter from the bank manager. Too much like hard work.

Nowadays, making a million looks easy. You can become a millionaire by answering just fifteen general knowledge questions posed by Chris

1

Tarrant. Or by the simple act of picking six numbers from forty-nine in the National Lottery.

The chances of doing so may be pretty limited. Millions ring into the *Who Wants to Be a Millionaire?* hotline, but only ten make it on to each programme and just two or three get a shot at answering the questions. It took two years for the show to produce its first millionaire. By late 2000, just over 1,000 people, less than 0.002 per cent of the population, had become millionaires by winning the jackpot on the Lottery.

Neither a game show like *Who Wants to Be a Millionaire?* nor the National Lottery would have been possible twenty years ago. Government rules did not allow them and it is probable that public opinion would not have accepted the concept. In those days, wealth was to be accumulated by effort, rather than luck (and to be redistributed by taxation, where possible). Gambling was a temptation from which the vulnerable had to be protected.

But the restrictions on quiz show prizes and on gambling have been swept away. It is now possible to gamble at any time of the day or night – from your personal computer, digital TV or mobile phone. With a spread bet, you can potentially make (and lose) thousands of pounds in a day on the basis of just one gamble. And those who miss out on games of chance have had another opportunity to make a million in recent years – the stock market.

In late 1999 and early 2000, it seemed that ordinary investors could make their fortunes by picking the right shares at the right time. Some small company stocks were rising by several hundred per cent in a day. In one week in December 1999, you could have turned £11,000 into a million if you had invested on successive days in the small companies Culver Holdings, Lionheart, Pordum Foods and Bolton International. Such returns lured many investors into the stock market: share turnover virtually doubled overnight in late 1999.

A new breed of investor emerged, who thought that making money from the stock market was a cinch. 'From September to November 1999, they were absolutely convinced they could stroll across Galilee and the rest of us were boring farts,' said Justin Urquhart Stewart, a director of Barclays Stockbrokers.

At the same time, the newspapers were full of stories of people who had started their own internet companies and had sold them for millions without going through the tedious process of making a profit. It seemed that merely working for the right company, in however lowly a capacity, gave you the chance of becoming a millionaire thanks to the generosity of share option schemes.

This was all part of a trend towards greater extremes in wealth. The better off have been getting, well, better off. According to the *Sunday Times Rich List 2000*, the collective wealth of the top 1,000 people in the UK reached almost £146bn, a rise of £31bn, or 27 per cent, over 1999. That was the biggest rise in the twelve years that the newspaper had been compiling the list. The number of internet millionaires on the list had risen from ten to sixty-three over one year. There were twenty-six UK billionaires, compared with just nine in 1989.

In the UK, there were around 7,000 millionaires in 1983. By 1997, on the basis of Inland Revenue figures, that number had grown to 77,000. And in late 2000, the consultancy Datamonitor estimated that the number of millionaires had grown by a further 50 per cent over the preceding three years. If houses are excluded, the most wealthy 10 per cent of the population owned 63 per cent of total wealth in 1996, a figure that had risen from 57 per cent in 1976.[1] The top 1 per cent of the population owns 27 per cent of total non-housing wealth.

Wealth cannot be created out of thin air. Cash or shares are simply a claim on goods and services. New and lasting wealth requires the creation of real goods and services; it also means that the businesses that produce those goods and services must earn an economic return on the capital invested. If they do not, then easy money is not new wealth but a transfer of existing wealth. Those people who sell their shares at the top have simply taken money out of the pockets of those who bought.

Those who aim for easy money face a fundamental problem. It is the golden rule of finance that risk and reward go hand in hand. By aiming for higher returns, investors inevitably face higher risk. That leaves them liable to lose most, or all, of their money – and it also leaves investors more open to fraud. Ralph Waldo Emerson once said 'The more he mentioned his honour, the faster we counted our spoons.' When people start talking about easy money, it's time to keep a firm hand on your wallet.

Obviously, the entire population of Britain are not going to become millionaires overnight, except in the case of hyperinflation. A few will get rich, some obscenely so – the rest of us will have to muddle along. Most of the gold prospectors who rushed to the Klondike returned empty-handed, if they returned at all. In a boom-and-bust market like the 1920s, only those who sold at the peak became rich. But by definition most investors are not smart – the top of the market occurs when buying reaches its peak.

Some businesses appear to offer easy money – the film industry and sports have done so for years. But that money flows to just a few stars and top athletes. Those who have invested in such enterprises have done far less well. The sum total of human wealth does grow from year to year but it grows very slowly. So when some people are making out like bandits, the chances are that others are losing out.

The lottery/game show transfer is easy to see through. People realise that it is their money that is going into the winners' pockets, whether by buying the £1 ticket or by phoning the *Who Wants to Be a Millionaire?* contestants' line. (Of course, the show makes plenty of money from advertising but that cash also, eventually, comes from the pockets of consumers.) The National Lottery is also a transfer from losers to winners with the government, promoters, shopkeepers and various good causes taking their cut along the way. So why do people buy the tickets, especially when the odds are so much against them? Clearly they reason that it is worth staking £1 for the chance of winning £1m. The loss of £1 will not change their life at all; the gaining of £1m will enable them (or so they believe) to change it out of all recognition.

Many people would say that investing in the stock market is far more rational than buying a Lottery ticket. But it may not be so if investors approach the stock market with a Lottery mentality.

In the past, academics worked on the assumption that investors were rational people. Economic and financial models work better that way. But there is a growing body of evidence – which happens to chime with common sense – that people are far from rational in their investment decisions.

As one example, investors, and particularly men, are overconfident about their abilities to pick the right shares. One academic study[2] found that men trade 45 per cent more often than women (and single men trade 67 per cent more often than single women). Trading costs money and reduces returns – in the case of the study, it meant that male investors underperformed females by around 1 percentage point a year. All that trading is clearly not rational. 'Rational investors trade only if the expected gains exceed transaction costs. Overconfident investors overestimate the precision of their information and thereby the expected gains of trading,' the study concluded.

One can get rich from the stock market, but the cold hard truth is that it is likely to be a slow process. And it will get even slower. After the long bull run in equities during the 1980s and 1990s, the chances are that returns will be lower, not higher, in future – just as more people are getting interested in the market.

The best approach is to 'buy and hold'. Save, and keep saving, a substantial part of your income for twenty or thirty years and the chances are that you will have done very well at the end of it. But few people have the patience for that. They want the money now, not when they are sixty. So they tend to invest in 'get rich quick' stocks. They follow fads and construct 'castles in the air', a trend that dates all the way back to the South Sea Bubble in the eighteenth century. Twenty or thirty years ago, such people would have invested in nickel or diamond mines; stock market lore says that the definition of a mine is 'a hole in the ground with a liar standing at the top'.

The internet is a classic instance of a fad. It is something about which people can make extravagant claims. It has a jargon of its own that makes it slightly mysterious – and thus harder to analyse. But it is much more immediate than a diamond mine; its benefits are something that people can experience for themselves.

Perhaps the internet is unique in history, however, in its twin appeal. Not only do people want to invest in companies that do business on the internet, but the internet by itself makes it easier for people to invest. You can trade shares with a click of the mouse and discover the latest financial news and market statistics at the same time as traders in City dealing rooms. In the language of California, investors have become 'empowered'.

This is good and bad. Private investors have been ignored or patronised by the professional community for too long. But making it easier to trade shares has encouraged the tendency to trade more often, a habit that is only likely to enrich stockbrokers. Day trading, a practice imported from the US, is a particularly pernicious habit – research has shown that 70 per cent of day traders lose money. 'The only way to make money from day trading is to write a book about it,' says Jeremy King of ProShare, an organisation that aims to encourage share ownership.

And the sheer newness of the internet makes it easy for investors to be blinded by bullshit. If the whole world is changing, why should old-fashioned stuff like profits (or even sales) matter any more? Why not pay 65p for a company with assets of just 2p a share as some investors did with Oxygen, a new issue in early 2000?

The Techmark 100 index – a sort of technology equivalent of the Footsie – started at 2,421 on 4 November 1999. By March 2000 – a period of just four months – it had reached 5,753. Tech investors had more than doubled their investment – easy money indeed.

Many stocks did far better than just double. Durlacher, once a fairly tiny stockbroker, recast itself as an internet group, with stakes in companies such as 365, the sports website. Its shares rose 6,000 per cent over the course of 1999; an investment of just £1,000 would have turned into £61,000 in twelve months.

There was not much logic in the rise. At its peak, Durlacher had a market value of more than £2bn, compared with a stated asset value on its books (its stakes in other internet companies) of just £14m. At the time, however, few people were interested in fundamentals. They just wanted a slice of the action. 'The media and websites were fuelling the idea that shares could double in a short time. Investors felt there was a boom in which there could be no downside,' recalls Ross Greenwood, the editor of *Shares* magazine. 'People saw investing as a way to make a quick buck and it was – for a while,' says Tony Hobman of the Money Channel, a financial TV network.

Investor optimism was understandable. By the time of dotcom mania in late 1999 and early 2000, it had been a quarter of a century since the last bear market in equities. Over that period, most people have been tempted into the stock market in one of three ways – privatisations, employee share options and demutualisations. The first two of those offered almost guaranteed profits and the third was almost literally free money[3] – investors were simply given the shares. Investing in shares did seem an easy business. So when the internet came along, it seemed like a no-brainer. A new technology that was going to change the world, how could it fail to make money? Anyone who didn't understand that just didn't 'get it'.

Journalists are paid to be cynical, but of course cynicism can be taken too far. It is easy to be a stick-in-the-mud and miss the significance of new inventions. Once one gets past thirty, conservatism tends to set in – new music no longer has a tune and you can't make out the words, new fashions look ridiculous, new gadgets are a fad and a waste of money. We get fed up with learning and adapting, we get comfortable with our existing tastes and habits and we simply cannot be bothered to make the effort to change.

Some people veer to the other extreme. They herald each new invention, each new fad, as the greatest thing since Mr Hovis learned to wield a knife. Thirty years ago, people believed supersonic travel would be the flight choice of millions. People would be going to the Moon for holidays. The roads would be jammed with Sinclair C5s.

The answer, as so often, is somewhere in the middle. Some new inventions do change the world. The twentieth century had plenty – the aeroplane, nuclear power, the personal computer, television and so on. Some people would put the internet in that category. But, even if it is, the key thought to keep in mind is: *just because it's a brilliant invention, that doesn't mean it's a brilliant business.* The reason for this is pretty straightforward. High sales do not make high profits. High profits result from being able to sell goods at a price considerably greater than the cost of producing them.

When businessmen spot a new growth business, they all want to get into it. That creates more competition in the market, driving prices down. Profit margins fall sharply. Even the pioneers lose their edge. In some cases, so many companies enter the business that the entire industry can lose money for a while. Indeed, if governments decide to back companies as a symbol of 'national pride', the sector can be almost permanently loss-making.

Take airlines. If you look back at the twentieth century, one of the great social and economic changes was the growth of airline travel. But Warren Buffett, the great US investor, once calculated that the sum total of all airline profits since the birth of the industry had been zero. Almost every national government has supported its own airline, or restricted the ability of other nations' airlines to compete. That has ensured the existence of far more airline businesses than the market can support – the result, fantastic growth in usage but permanently low profits.

This is true for a lot of businesses. New technological developments usually bring their greatest benefits to the general population, not to the investment community. Since there are a lot more people than there are investors, this is a good thing. Of course, some investors will become extremely rich out of a new development, but that will usually be because they invested when nobody else was interested, prices were cheap and the risks looked high. By the time a technological development hits the Sunday supplements, the easy money has probably been made.

It is true that, unlike the National Lottery, the stock market is not a zero-sum game. Share prices rise over time so it is perfectly possible for everyone to become gradually wealthier by investing. But this wealth has to bear some relationship to fundamentals, the assets and profits of the corporate sector, and those fundamentals can be obscured by the ups and downs of share prices.

The nature of wealth

Wealth can be a slightly nebulous concept. A thousand years ago, wealth came in the form of precious metals and jewels, even though such things provide no nourishment, warmth or shelter. Paper currency replaced metal as the basis for wealth, although its only practical use would be as a fuel. In this century, we have rapidly moved on so that wealth is merely an entry on a computer.

In all these cases, of course, the key is public confidence. Provided other people will accept your form of wealth in return for the stuff you do need – food, clothes, oil – then it *is* wealth. A fifteenth-century merchant would have looked askance at your credit card; the Tesco checkout operator would be baffled if you produced a gold nugget to pay for your groceries.

If you look carefully at your bank notes, you will see that they bear the legend 'I promise to pay the bearer on demand the sum of five pounds (or ten pounds etc.)'. This dates back to the days when a paper note was merely a claim on 'real' wealth in the form of gold or silver. Nowadays that promise is meaningless, as anyone turning up at the Bank of England with a bagful of fivers will soon discover.

But it doesn't matter. Shops are happy to accept your notes because they, in turn, are able to pass them on to others in return for goods and services. They are equally happy to receive debit and credit cards but they are no longer so happy about accepting cheques, for the very good reason that banks will not guarantee to honour cheques above a certain sum.

Many people hold a lot of their wealth in the form of cash or 'near-cash' items such as bank deposits. Those who want their wealth to grow more rapidly invest in other assets – but again the key for them is to pick an asset that will be accepted as wealth by others. One obvious answer is physical wealth – property, fine art, or jewellery.

Financial assets are widely accepted as a form of wealth but they are much more valuable if they are easily traded – investors will be more keen to invest in a company whose shares are traded on a stock market (and thus can be sold quickly when needed) than in a company whose shares are privately held.

Equities, like most other financial assets, have a daily trading price that we can use to calculate their 'worth' or 'value'. The leading 300 companies in the European stock markets, for example, were worth 6.3trillion euros at the end of January 2000. But if all the owners of shares had wanted to sell their holdings, they clearly would not have raised anything like 6.3trillion euros. Who would there be left to buy?

Like the value of money, the value of equities depends crucially on confidence – in this case that the supply of buyers and sellers will remain roughly in balance. At the height of a bull market very few people want to sell and many want to buy, so prices move sharply higher. The value of all equities will rise, whether they are traded or not. Similarly in a bear market, the absence of buyers will mean that all prices fall – and even those who do not sell their shares will feel poorer.

The above may seem obvious but it is crucially important. How do investors get a return from equities? The answer is in two ways. The first is in the form of income, from the dividends that some companies pay out of their annual profits. The second is in the form of capital gain. But, of course, the realisation of capital gain requires the investor to find someone else who will buy the asset. That investor, in turn, must presumably anticipate making a further capital gain and finding a third investor willing to purchase the shares. The whole population cannot sell at once. We cannot, as a nation, make ourselves richer simply by buying and selling shares any more than we can construct a viable economy simply by taking in each other's washing.

So let us get back to our internet companies. Normally, companies are valued in terms of the assets they own, the profits they produce or the dividends they pay. But in the case of many internet companies, they had barely any assets, paid no dividends and made a loss. Investors bought such shares in the hope of *future* assets, profits and dividends.

Clearly, internet companies produce wealth to the extent that they sell goods and services. But to the extent that this wealth is sustainable then they must produce a return on investors' capital. If they do not produce such a return, then eventually the capital will run out and the company will go bust. And if they do not produce any return, then the 'wealth' created by their flotation on the stock market has not added to overall economic output – it simply represents a transfer from investors to the company's employees, consumers and suppliers.

Say a company floats on the market at £100m on the back of its future profits prospects. However, with our crystal ball, we can see that future profits do not justify a worth of £100m but of £50m, or even zero. Eventually, the market will realise this and the money will disappear. Where will that money go? When a new company floats, it can either issue new shares to raise new capital and expand the business, or existing shareholders can sell out to realise a profit. Normally, a new issue involves a bit of both, with greater emphasis on capital-raising. (Existing investors are expected to sell only part of their stake to counter the obvious question: if they are selling, why should anyone else be buying?)

In our worthless business, to the extent that original investors sell out on flotation, and new investors buy into the shares at the flotation price, there will have been a direct transfer of wealth between the two. (Of course, new investors may be able to sell before the bad news sinks in; so the next round of investors will bear the bulk of the losses.) Similarly, to the extent that founders exercise their share options and sell out later on, their 'wealth' will have come from the pockets of those investors who buy the new shares.

What about companies that have raised capital to expand their businesses? If the expansion plans fail, this also represents a transfer of wealth. Most internet companies seem to have spent the bulk of their capital on advertising, with the aim of establishing their brand names. Pets.com was reported to have spent $179 on marketing for every customer it acquired. So you could view these businesses as a conduit for the transfer of wealth from equity investors to advertisers. Boo.com, an online fashion house, failed after spending £90m or so of investor capital; the receiver found that the value of the remaining assets was just £1m.

Huge sums were involved in the launch of dotcom businesses. According to PriceWaterhouseCoopers, the accountancy group, venture capital investments in internet-related companies rose from $176m in 1995 to just under $20bn in 1999. Initial public offerings in net companies raised $75.2bn in the five years to November 2000, according to CommScan, a research service; net companies raised a further $51.6bn after they came to the market.

As fast as money flowed into these businesses, much of it flowed out. Some $5.3bn went in fees to investment banks; $22.6bn went to insiders selling shares. A lot went to customers, in the form of cheap prices. A study by McKinsey, the management consultants, found that in the fourth quarter of 1999, Drugstore.com lost $16.42 on every order for non-prescription goods it sold while e-Toys lost $4.04 on each order it received.

This kind of madness was never going to last for ever. In the UK, the collapse of Boo.com brought to an end, for the moment at least, the period when investors viewed all dotcom stocks with starry eyes. Even before then, when they read about seventeen-year-olds becoming internet millionaires from their bedrooms, sensible investors should have begun to worry.

Easy money was made, and then lost again. At their peak 2000 price levels, the magnificent seven UK technology stocks of ARM, Baltimore, Bookham, Durlacher, Freeserve, Psion and QXL.com had a market value of £40.7bn. By early April 2001, their collective market value had dropped to £5.6bn, with the starkest drop seen at QXL, whose value fell from £2.5bn to £40m.

The bulk of that fall in value simply represents a paper loss to investors, including executives and venture capitalists, who held the shares throughout the period. But it is likely that billions of pounds were lost by pension funds, insurance companies and small investors who bought at the top of the market. It is easy to shrug your shoulders and say that: 'a fool and his money are soon parted.' But that is too simplistic a view. Stock Exchange rules were altered so that companies without either profits or a track record could come to the market. Small investors were encouraged by stockbrokers and the media to buy such stocks. Those who lost money in the dotcom crash may be discouraged from investing in equities again – making it more difficult for them to enjoy a decent income in their old age and for other companies to raise capital.

Dotcom mania was one sign of a remarkable social change – how making money and talking about money is much more acceptable than it used to be. The book also focuses on a remarkable technological change, how the internet made it easier for people to start new businesses and to get involved in the stock market. And in part, it is a story of economic change, and the issue of whether a 'new era' has dawned in the developed world.

This is not the work of a Luddite. I do not think that the internet is a pointless invention; I feel no social outrage if people become rich; I believe it is, on balance, a good thing if more people get involved in the stock market.

Bur it's worth analysing those changes with a sceptical, but not dogmatically negative, eye. The cultural shift will last much longer than most dotcom stocks. So I hope this book may be useful as recording the new era's early moments. And of the immense potential, and wishful thinking, that accompanied them.

1

Trading Places

The stock is the horse, the stockbroker the jockey,
the punter is the shareholder.

Private investor

The alarm goes at 7.30 in the morning. You listen to the news headlines on Radio 4 and wander downstairs in your dressing gown. You login to your favourite website to check the latest financial headlines. At 8 a.m., the UK market opens and you start trading. Forget George Soros, forget Warren Buffett; today you're going to kick butt.

Sounds good? Certainly, it seems better than working. No struggling through the rush hour, no boss to keep you in line. Just your money and your wits against the rest of the world.

John Delaney was a private investor who traded heavily in shares in late 1999 and early 2000. 'I started buying tech shares that I didn't really understand on the basis of newsletters like *Quantum Leap*,' he recalls. 'But because they did well, I started to do some digging of my own. I was trading on credit and more often than not I was closing out with gains. Some days I made £2,000 – that was serious money – and I started really getting into it. Sometimes I spent half the night researching shares.'

He used the in-and-out tactics characteristic of day traders – people who buy and sell shares in search of short-term gains. 'As things went up, I sold and put the money into something else. It was hard to find shares that weren't winning at that time – some shares were going up 50–60 per cent in a day. I bought and sold shares like Geo Interactive when it was down at 42p. I'd buy it, make 20, 30, 40 per cent and be into the next thing.'

Day traders like Mr Delaney are common in the US, but they are still pretty rare in the UK. That's not too surprising. If you are hoping to live off your investments, you need to have a large sum to play with. Say you want to earn £25,000 a year. If you aim to make a 10 per cent return on your investments (and that's pretty optimistic over the long run if inflation is 2 per cent), you'll need a lump sum of £250,000. Few people have that kind of lump sum and even fewer of those would want to devote their time to playing the markets.

In the US, some day traders gather in centres where they can get all the financial information they need and they can sit, staring at their computer screens, all day. It is a concept not far removed from the vast electronic gaming rooms of Las Vegas, where gamblers play one-armed bandits and video poker all night.

Without reaching the extremes of the US, there does seem to have been a quantum leap in the involvement of UK private investors in the stock market over the last couple of years. More people are following the markets, more are investing and more are trading. The phenomenon really became noticeable in the winter of 1999. There was a sharp increase in the number of trades done each day on the stock market – one indicator of private investor activity – from 75,000 to 110,000 and then to 140,000 in the spring.

What sparked the change? The Techmark forum for technology companies was launched on the London stock exchange in November 1999. All it did was lump technology companies together in one index. In theory, it should have made no difference at all to share prices. But the extra publicity and attention seemed to draw private investors into the technology sector.

At the same time in the US, the Nasdaq market – largely but not exclusively based on technology stocks – took off, with its Composite index rising from 1,419 in October 1998 to 5,048 in March 2000, a 256 per cent gain in eighteen months. In Europe, private investors flocked to buy technology stocks such as internet service providers Terra Networks and Tiscali.

The pace seemed to quicken even further in early 2000. Three-quarters of a million people registered to buy shares in an internet investment website, Interactive Investor. There was enormous publicity about the flotation of Lastminute.com, an online booking agent with two glamorous founders. Two investment-based cable TV channels were launched – the Money Channel and Simply Money.

Behind all this, a fundamental factor may have been at work, the availability of money. Despite the title of this book, it is not a treatise on monetary policy. But it now seems clear that the world's central banks played their part in fuelling this sudden surge in the stock market.

It's hard to recall it now, but lots of people really did believe that the world economy might collapse at the end of 1999 because of the millennium bug. This software glitch was caused by a space-saving measure used in the early days of computing; years were recorded in two digits rather than four, 99 instead of 1999. As the year 2000 approached, the worry was that computers would simply freeze when confronted with the year 00, or they would assume the year was 1900 and decide, for example, that pensions should be cancelled because the recipients had yet to be born.

The scare stories were legion. Perhaps they were simply a wonderful excuse for software programmers to earn fees or perhaps the reprogramming work did help us avoid disaster. We shall never know. But part of a central bank's job is to avert crisis and the US Federal Reserve and the Bank of England decided that it would be a disaster if panicky consumers, fearing computer breakdowns, all decided to withdraw their money from the banks. So they arranged for lots of cash to be pumped into the financial system. In the last two months of 1999, the US central bank expanded its reserves at an annualised rate of 300 per cent. In the first four months of 2000, it contracted reserves at an annualised rate of 60 per cent.[1]

Speculative bubbles through the ages have depended on two things: lots of available credit and a plausible 'get rich quick' scheme. In the eighteenth century, it was the lure of lucrative trade with the 'South Seas'; in the nineteenth century, it was railway mania. In late 1999, it just so happened that the central banks pumped money into the global economy at a time when there was lots of publicity concerning the marvels of the internet.

The internet was the modern King Midas; everything it touched seemed to turn to gold. And it caught the imagination of the public. Take the views of one investor, Liz Cameron: 'I think people have got interested because of the huge amounts of money being made during the dotcom era and, like myself, once in there, you're a bit hooked. Also with the ever-increasing wealth of information and opinion available on the net – it's never been easier. People like myself had no understanding of the close world of stock market trading and the combination of the above factors has, I feel, opened a window on the world.'

'There was clearly a focus on the internet,' said Jeremy King of ProShare, an organisation designed to promote wider share ownership. 'People saw the returns being gained by net companies and there was a belief that everything to do with the net would make money. People read stories about other people doing well.'

'What sparked the transformation was that people could see the technology stocks doing well,' says Nigel Reynolds, a director of stockbroker Charles Schwab (Europe). 'Some institutions were investing in ten start-ups in the hope that one would succeed. For a couple of months, you couldn't go wrong as far as technology stocks were concerned.'

There was also a widespread feeling that it was almost their right to make easy money in the modern world. The average investor thought: 'Other people are making a fortune – why not me?'

And this was not boring old investment of the kind that involves locking away shares in a drawer for ten years. This was gambling, pure and simple. 'They don't see it as investment, they see it as a game,' says Justin Urquhart Stewart of Barclays Stockbrokers.

A change of generation

How did Britons suddenly get so enthusiastic about owning shares? My mum won't invest in shares at all – she regards them as far too risky. When she was growing up, her father lost his business in the great depression of the 1930s, severely reducing the family circumstances. That kind of experience puts you off risk for life.

Bitter experience taught many Britons of her generation the same lesson. Shares were a bit too hot for most people's blood. The high personal tax rates put in place after the Second World War played their part as well. At one point, the top rate on earned income was 83 per cent and any unearned income was taxed at 15 per cent on top for a combined rate of 98 per cent. (Such a high tax on 'unearned' income is entirely irrational in macroeconomic terms. Why is it better for people to spend their money than to save it? Without savings, there would be no investment and the economy would never grow.)

Instead of investing in shares, it was far better for the wealthy to become members of the Lloyds insurance market (the tax advantages were great and the well-publicised losses didn't appear until the last decade) or, for less affluent people, to buy a life insurance policy, where the premiums were tax-deductible.

According to ProShare, the proportion of the stock market owned by individuals fell from 65.8 per cent in 1957 to 16.5 per cent by 1997.[2]

But that figure doesn't tell the whole story. First of all, the collective interest of Britons in the stock market rose steadily over the period, thanks to the savings locked away in pension funds and insurance companies. Britons did not own shares directly but the health of the stock market still determined a lot of people's long-term wealth.

Secondly, share ownership may have become less deep but it did become more broadly spread, thanks to privatisations and the demutualisation of the building societies. In 1979, just 3 million people owned shares, by 1998 it was 12 million after a brief high of 15 million in 1997.

Most of these people were just dabbling in the market. According to ProShare, 48 per cent of investors owned just one share in 1997. Only 6 per cent owned eleven or more, the minimum thought necessary to create a diversified portfolio. (Diversification limits the possibility for bad news at one company to cause significant damage to an investor's savings.) 'We had the width of share ownership but we didn't have the depth,' says Richard Hunter of NatWest Stockbrokers.

The privatisations laid the groundwork for the recent burst of enthusiasm for share ownership. Remember the marketing slogan for British Gas – 'If you see Sid, tell him'? Newspapers still occasionally refer to private investors as Sids. Privatisations got investors used to the idea of owning shares – and to the practical paraphernalia such as share certificates, dividend cheques and annual reports. They also got investors used to the idea that share ownership was a one-way bet – the offers were deliberately priced at a low level to ensure that the issues were a success. Profits may only have been in the tens or hundreds of pounds, but at least they were profits.

The process was given a further kick in the mid-1990s by the wave of demutualisations of building societies and insurance companies, which passed shares to 29 per cent of the UK population. After an initial surge, the shares of companies like the Halifax did not perform that well, but as far as investors were concerned it was all 'free money'. Unlike the privatisations, they did not have to put up money to buy the shares.

Share ownership is still a minority occupation in the UK but it is more widespread than you might think. By 1998, 27 per cent of UK adults owned shares, compared with 40 per cent in the US and 53 per cent in Sweden (but just 6.4 per cent in Germany). Unsurprisingly, share ownership was skewed towards the better-off – 44 per cent of all AB people were share-holders compared with 13 per cent of DEs. But the proportion of C1s, C2s and DEs owning shares had all increased since 1993.

Broken down by age and sex, more males (30 per cent) than females (24 per cent) owned shares and share ownership was most common among the over sixty-fives. By TV area, share ownership was most common in the Meridian region (in the south and south-east) and least common in the HTV (Wales) and Tyne TV regions (north-east England).

Justin Urquhart Stewart of Barclays Stockbrokers has devised a whole taxonomy system for the UK private investor. 'George represents the 2 million shareholders who existed before privatisations. He owned shares because Mummy and Daddy had passed them down and he had his portfolio looked after by a stockbroker.

'Sid bought privatisations and Super Sids bought them for the whole family. Henry was the investor who started trading after that. He followed advice in the *Telegraph* and the *Mail*. Super Henries knew a lot about a dozen or so stocks, probably more than their broker. And Electric Henries emerged in September 1999. They were twenty years younger than the rest. They didn't necessarily trade over the net but they did have access to it. They weren't interested in investing but in punting in stocks we'd never heard of.'

The new brokers

Available credit gave investors the means to invest in shares; the internet and the prevailing culture gave them the motive; but stockbrokers gave them the opportunity.

Stockbrokers have never had a great image among the British public. Ask the average man to describe a broker and the chances are that he will use terms such as posh, rich and, of course, pinstripe suit. Many people have in the past refrained from investing in shares because they felt they would be 'looked down on' by brokers for their lack of wealth and knowledge.

And it is true that the traditional stockbroking community was not really interested in investors whose holdings were worth just a few hundred pounds or so. Such people would trade only rarely and in small amounts. Traditional brokers tended to have high charges and be interested in people with at least six figures to invest.

But the privatisations of the 1980s created a niche in the market – suddenly there were millions of new investors who owned small amounts of shares. The company that moved fastest to exploit it was Sharelink, a Birmingham-based group that decided to specialise at the smaller end of the market (it is now owned by US broker Charles Schwab). It offered a cut-rate postal service for those who wanted to cash in their privatisation gains.

The new breed of brokers tended to be *execution-only* firms. This meant that they restricted their service to buying and selling shares on the investors' behalf; they would not offer advice, or manage an investor's portfolio. This allowed them to conduct deals at a very cheap rate – good news for the new breed of smaller investor. As of November 2000, for example, Hargreaves Lansdown was offering a commission of just £9.95, regardless of the size of the deal.

This is the 'can do' generation – when people have been taught that they can achieve anything if they put their mind to it. Take a TV advert for Sharepeople, an online stockbroker. It shows golfer Colin Montgomerie agonising over a pitch to the green. While he and his caddie are surveying the terrain, a spectator steps out of the crowd, plays the shot and lands the ball a few inches from the hole. The idea behind the ad is clear. Many people are put off the stock market, thinking it is only for the experts. But in fact, you can be a stock market star, with the help of the Sharepeople brokerage. The analogy may be rather more pointed than the stockbroker, and its advertising agency, intended. Yes, it is always possible, that an amateur might produce a better golf shot from a given position than Colin Montgomery. But 99 times out of 100, the professional would triumph. And the complete novice is far more likely to send his ball into the bunker, or take a divot out of the turf, than to produce a perfect shot.

When stock markets are surging, however, every investor appears to be a genius. The result was that even the new breed of stockbrokers, however, appeared to have been taken by surprise by the sudden surge in demand in late 1999. 'We first noticed the change in November,' says Nigel Reynolds of Charles Schwab. 'But trade often picks up in November and it wasn't until two weeks into December that we felt there was something different going on.'

The phone lines became continually jammed. There were reports of investors waiting up to forty minutes to get through – and share prices can move significantly over that kind of period. One client was even said to have suffered a heart attack while waiting to get through to make a trade.

'We realised that when people started coming back after New Year, it would be absolutely mad,' says Reynolds. 'We opened our new call centre in February when we had expected to open it in April. But due to the complexity of the phone calls we receive, we couldn't afford to just get people off the street. We had to give them a rigorous training programme.' Eventually, Schwab doubled its number of call centre staff.

People were talking about their share trades in the pub and at work. 'It was like the rumours of petrol shortages, the desire to trade spread like wildfire,' recalls Justin Urquhart Stewart of Barclays Stockbrokers.

Even before late 1999, there had been a steady upward trend in investor activity. Figures from Charterhouse Securities show that the average daily turnover in equities in 1997 was just under £2.4bn. In 1998, that increased to £2.7bn. Then there was a big jump to £3.9bn in 1999 and £5.3bn in the first nine months of 2000.

Net trading

Part of that increase was the result of trading over the internet. According to ComPeer, which keeps figures on the subject, the number of internet trades increased from 29,000 in the first quarter of 1999 to 51,000 in the second quarter, 151,000 in the third and 371,000 in the fourth. In the first quarter of 2000, there was a phenomenal jump to 930,000 trades.

The internet made it easy for anyone to find a broker. 'Five years ago, people would have wondered how to get a stockbroker. Do they advertise in the Yellow Pages?' recalls Tony Hobman of the Money Channel. Heavy TV and press advertising, plus the marvel of the internet search engine, made brokers such as E*Trade and Sharepeople easy to find.

Among the internet's many attractions is that it is an anonymous and democratic medium. You can deal without ever having to speak to another human; you can do it naked or in your scruffiest jeans and T-shirt. Once you are logged on, you can deal on the same basis as a Rothschild or a Rockefeller.

It still took a little time for investors to get the hang of trading on the net. Nigel Reynolds of Charles Schwab (Europe) says, 'We had started our internet trading service in April 1998. In 1999, we saw people were using the internet to look at their accounts but when they wanted to trade, they picked up the phone.'

Reynolds felt that investors were simply nervous about the system.

'They wanted to try the service but they wanted to try it for a deal worth hundreds of pounds, not thousands,' he says. But Schwab's minimum commission made the proportionate cost of a deal of £200 or so prohibitive.

So Charles Schwab took a gamble and offered free dealing over the internet for a month. That gave investors every incentive to try the system out; nothing is so attractive as a bargain. 'As an initiative, it was a great success,' says Reynolds. 'We saw phenomenal growth in existing customers converting to the net. And it didn't cost us a large amount.'

But the decisive factor in encouraging internet trading may well have been the difficulty investors had in reaching traditional brokers by telephone over the winter of 1999. Online dealing was instant and saved them the long musical interlude on the telephone.

Turnover slackened a bit after March 2000, when the Nasdaq market in the US suddenly began to fall. Some of the more speculative stocks that had surged in late 1999/early 2000 fell almost as quickly as they had risen. The number of internet trades dropped to 648,000 in the second quarter of 2000, but that still left activity twelve times higher than a year previously.

And according to Paul Lubbock of online broker DLJ Direct, the decline in online trading activity in the second quarter of 2000 was lower than that of the offline market. At the end of June 2000, the internet represented 19 per cent of total market trades, up from 1 per cent in the second quarter of 1999. In terms of numbers of internet-based accounts, there were 233,000 by the end of June 2000, compared with just 38,000 in September 1999.

Dealing on the net is very simple. I've done it myself (to sell Pearson shares acquired through my employer's savings scheme) and found it a little frightening to see how easy it was. I selected the symbol for Pearson shares, asked for a quote, and then clicked 'accept' when I saw the price. Within a second or two, the deal had gone through and I was committed to a transaction worth several thousand pounds. I could, just as easily, have spent all the proceeds with a few more clicks of the mouse.

The net's very openness means that brokers have to insist on safeguards. Most will now ask you to deposit money with them before you can buy shares. If you want to sell shares, they must have the certificates (they will be held in what is called a nominee account). You can see why they do this. Once you send the instructions to trade, they do the deal on your behalf. If you failed to pay up, or send the shares, they would be liable to meet the costs of the deal. Since, by the nature of the net, the broker will barely know you from Adam, this is not a risk they are willing to take.

There is also the risk, of course, that someone else might deal on your behalf. Thus, not only do you need to enter an identification number and passwords, but also the site will contain security features (software that encrypts the message rather like a telephone scrambling device) to prevent hackers from intercepting it.

As in other fields such as credit card transactions, battling fraud on the internet will doubtless become a constant evolutionary struggle in which criminals (and the mischievous) gradually learn to circumvent existing security measures, sparking a new approach from the industry.

Frequent trading

The evidence is that the ease of trading on the internet encourages investors to deal more often. A ProShare survey found that 58 per cent of those who had used the internet for trading had increased their level of activity. Those who had not registered with an online broker averaged twelve transactions per year; those who traded on the net averaged twenty. Over 20 per cent of those who had traded shares online had also bought and sold shares on the same day in order to make a short-term gain. In the US, home of internet trading, the average holding period for a share has now fallen to below ninety days.

Just because it has become easier to trade more often does not mean it is necessarily sensible to do so. Every time investors buy and sell shares, it costs them money. Some of those costs, particularly the commission charged by brokers, have fallen in the net era but others have not. There is still a spread between the buying and selling price of shares and in the UK there is still, at the time of writing, a 0.5 per cent stamp duty on share purchases.

Costs can be even greater if you are investing small sums in the first place. 'If you put £100 in a stock, by the time you've paid £15 commission and stamp duty and the spread, you're going to need to make 20 per cent just to break even,' says Richard Hunter of NatWest Stockbrokers. 'You've got to start with £500 as a minimum unit size.'

It's a bit like playing roulette. Every time the ball lands on zero or double zero, the house takes all the bets. That gives the house a cut of just under 3 per cent or just over 5 per cent depending on which system is used.

Even if you keep betting conservatively on red or black, that edge to the house slowly and remorselessly absorbs your cash. If you play for long enough, the odds are that your money will disappear.

Let us say that it costs around 2–3 per cent every time an investor deals. If every share in the portfolio is traded just once a year, that will reduce the potential return by 2–3 per cent. That is equivalent to wiping out the entire dividend income at current market levels. That 2–3 per cent figure is also close to the historic margin between the returns achieved from holding cash or bonds, and those available from owning shares (the actual average is around 4 per cent a year).

Frequent trading tilts the odds of success against an investor beating the returns available from cash, or in fact making a profit at all. Indeed, stock-brokers can be accused of 'churning' if they deal too often on a client's be-half – the assumption of the regulators is that the broker is more interested in earning large commissions than in seeing their client's money grow. And frequent trading is even harder when markets are falling. In the UK, most day traders have to bet that prices will go up, because it is very diffi-cult to go short (sell shares you do not own in the hope of buying them back at a lower price).

That made life extremely difficult for day traders when tech stocks started to fall in March 2000. 'At one point I was up nearly £1m but a lot of that disappeared,' recalls John Delaney. 'I reduced my holdings but I didn't get out completely. I saw it [the market] was very high but we still thought it could go higher. These new technologies were going to make so much money.'

When share prices fell sharply, Delaney suffered accordingly. 'I lost £250,000 in a day when I couldn't get out. Some shares got hit 70–80 per cent.' But it was not all bad news. Although Mr Delaney lost some of the gains he made at the peak of the market, he still feels he has done ex-tremely well out of his investments, which have helped finance new homes and an expensive car.

Delaney was one of the lucky ones. 'I've got friends that lost £300,000–400,000 in the market and are struggling to pay the gas bill,' he says. 'I have a friend in Yorkshire – a pig farmer – who was trading shares. The Ferrari brochure arrived on the day the market collapsed.'

Debs Harris was a private investor who was day trading in the equity market in early 2000, largely in technology shares. 'I went on holiday in March and when I came back, I had lost a substantial amount,' she recalls.

'Day trading is not worth it in the current market. You just see shares going against you. Quite a few day traders I know have got decimated portfolios and have just left it. You can't just depend on trading for income unless you're an expert or you're lucky.'

She advises anyone who wants to take up day trading not to risk real money at first. 'Watch the market and put together your own strategy. I hate to use clichés, but do not invest what you can't afford to lose.'

So why do so many people trade so often? Indeed, why does a practice like day trading occur at all? One reason is investor psychology. Just as most car owners think they are above-average drivers, most people who trade stocks and shares think they are above-average investors. Not for them the standard return of 6–7 per cent a year. They imagine that they will earn a lot more.

A study by Brad Barber and Terrance Odean at the University of California in Davis[3] found that the investors who were most likely to switch to trading online were young men with high incomes and a preference for investing in small-growth stocks with high market risk. After going online, they trade more actively, more speculatively and less profitably than before – lagging the market by more than 3 per cent annually. 'Most investors will benefit from a slow trading, buy-and-hold strategy,' said the academics. 'Trigger-happy investors are prone to shooting themselves in the foot.'

Barber and Odean's research only covered the US, but it seems likely that UK online traders follow the same pattern. ProShare's research found that investors using the internet for share dealings are more likely to have 'higher risk' portfolios.

When, in early-to-mid 2000, I polled readers of the *FT* about their investment views,[4] most expected annual returns in the double digits with some looking for as much as 50 per cent a year. That kind of return would have beaten the legendary hedge fund manager George Soros at his best – and Soros had the advantage of using borrowed money (which enhances returns at the expense of increased risk).

It was remarkable how many of the private investors who replied had very ambitious targets. Stephen Rivett said, 'I started watching the FTSE and noticed that average gains of 25 per cent per year (minus dealing charges) were achievable.' Lorenz Nwachuku expected an annual return of 20–50 per cent. Joe Cittern said, 'My timescales have moved out so instead of doubling in a year, I might now expect doubling in two years' (i.e. an annual return of 50 per cent).

The golden rule, indeed, of finance is that greater reward involves greater risk. If you want to earn 20 per cent a year, you will not do so, over the long term, by backing big companies in the FTSE 100 index. You will have to gamble on highly speculative stocks. By doing so, you increase the risk of losing money.

Investors read about a few wonder stocks like ARM Holdings or Durlacher, whose value has risen ten- or even a thousandfold.[5] They start to fantasise about earning such returns themselves, without thinking that their chances of picking such stocks is very low.

You can understand the rationale of such people. If you have, say, £5,000 to invest, then earning 6–7 per cent a year will never make you rich. You would only double your money every ten to twelve years. So if you started at twenty-five, you would not reach £1m until you were around a hundred years old, a bit too late to enjoy it. Better to speculate with the money, investors reason, in the hope they achieve the stock market equivalent of winning the Lottery.

So that means going for the high-risk stocks, rather than safe and reliable companies like utilities. 'It's a much sexier story to look at a dotcom stock that will double overnight than to invest in an old economy stock that will only double over the much longer term,' says Richard Hunter of NatWest Stockbrokers. It's a very similar philosophy to that followed by those who like just an occasional flutter on the horses. Betting on the favourite, at odds of evens or worse, doesn't seem worth it – the potential gain seems so small. So gamblers gravitate towards outsiders at 33-1 or 100-1. In fact, experienced gamblers will tell you that betting on favourites is the only way you are likely to make money from betting over the long run. Horses that race at odds of 100-1 almost never win – they certainly win a lot less than 1 per cent of all races.

Indeed, many investors explicitly think of the stock market in gambling terms. One investor, Simon Gordon, told me that 'having money in the market is better than in the bank because in the bank it is like watching paint dry. It [the market] is gambling and full of risk. It lets you see the future and how society is constructed now. I like the analogy of horse racing – the stock is the horse, the stockbroker the jockey, the punter is the shareholder – with companies ranging from thoroughbreds in the classics [FTSE 100] to handicappers [midcap] and sellers [smallcap].

'As a punter you can be into the art of investing or be a total speculator hungry for a fast buck, a person lost in the philosophy of complete greed, divorced from contemplation and beauty. Investing is a practice to be learnt over a lifetime, not a quick screw and then on to the next thing. It is a long learning curve.'

'The only way to make serious gains is to bet on a few big winners,' says Joe Cittern, who got seriously interested in the stock market in the mid 1990s, having kept his money in the building society till then. 'You won't make big gains if you diversify into fifty companies and sit in 50 per cent cash most of the time.' Joe claims to be one of the lucky ones, having seen his investments grow tenfold to date.[6]

Joe is the exception, rather than the rule. Imagine that you had a national coin-tossing competition in which every single Briton was entered. To get through to the next round, all you would have to do is toss heads. So, there being 55 million Britons, you would expect around 27.5 million to survive the first round, 13.75 million the second round and so on. After about nineteen rounds, you would expect to see 105 Britons still in the competition.

One can just imagine the newspapers running features on the remaining players, who would cite their wrist action, hours of practice or devotion to their mothers as the reason they had successfully thrown heads nineteen times in a row. But, of course, the next time they throw the coin, they would still have a 50–50 chance of getting heads.

Similarly with investment, you will always get some investors who beat the market. But plenty of academic research suggests this is more often due to luck than skill – past performance, as they say, is no guide to the future.

The psychological trait of overconfidence, however, means that investors, like the champion coin-tossers, will start to believe in their own ability. When they make money, it is due to their own skill. When they lose money it is down to bad luck. They will then trade more, not less, increase their costs and reduce their returns.

Investors also tend to follow irrational trading strategies. In particular, they find it very difficult to take a loss. Taking a loss forces someone to admit they have made a mistake. Far better to hang on to the share, in the hope that it will come good. In contrast, investors are often eager to sell shares where they have made a profit – to bank their gains. The inevitable result is that their portfolios become riddled with failures while they sell the successes too early.

This psychological tendency, known as loss aversion, has been documented. A study by Terrance Odean of the University of California in

Davis[7] found that private investors in the US are 1.5–2 times more likely to sell their winning stocks than to sell their losers.

Mark Eccleston is a TV presenter who started investing in individual shares in 1999. 'I was lucky in that I had one share that did very well, sportingbet.com. I made a fair amount of money out of that and put it all into similar types of stock such as Cube8. I bought that one at 28p, now it's 2.5p.'[8]

'All of my stocks are around 30 per cent of what they were. I was a bit inexperienced and I felt that, having taken a loss, I couldn't sell. It got to the stage where it's not worth selling. I might as well hang on for ten years. Having bought at the top, you don't want to sell at the bottom. But I'm not going to put any more money into shares.'

As another investor said to me: 'Losses, like profits, only become actual when you sell.'

No shortage of opinion

Investors have much better access to financial information than they used to – whether it is about share prices, company data or the latest market news. No longer do they have to rely on the information that dribbled out from an old-fashioned stockbroker, who usually had a hundred clients to deal with and very little time to speak to each individual.

The BBC runs regular updates on the financial world in its breakfast programmes on radio and TV. The national newspapers now have far bigger City and personal finance sections than they did twenty years ago (they find the advertising revenue very attractive). CNBC Europe and Bloomberg have been running financial cable TV channels for several years; as already noted, the Money Channel and Simply Money started broadcasting on digital TV in early 2000. And financial websites proliferate – from UK Invest to MoneyGuru to Motley Fool UK.

This has given private investors more confidence to trade in the market. Billy Fitzgerald started investing in the stock market in 1995, having previously kept his savings in government bonds and bank deposits. He decided to invest because of 'inexpensive and easy access to timely information. The widespread availability of statistical and financial information in searchable databases gives the individual investor a "fighting chance" in the financial markets.'

What Fitzgerald describes is both a good and bad development. The good news is that private investors are no longer completely 'out of the loop', dealing on a disadvantaged basis compared with their institutional counterparts. But the bad news is that the sheer volume of coverage of the stock market these days also makes it more tempting to trade. Much of the advice available is contradictory (this is inevitable; every time you buy a share, someone else is selling. If you think it is going to go up, they must think it is going to go down). So it is easy to become like a sofa, which retains the impression of the last person to sit on it. The *Sunday Times* tips Vodafone so you purchase the shares on Monday. But then a website says that Vodafone is losing market share and BT is the better buy. So you call your broker and sell Vodafone and buy BT. All the while the costs mount up.

Rather like gambling, the constant movement of share prices and torrent of news can become addictive. 'When I went on to the internet, I looked at one of the financial sites and I started to get obsessed about watching the graphs. I was visiting the site two or three times a day,' says Mark Eccleston.

The sheer volume of information available may well be a case of 'a little knowledge is a dangerous thing'. Investment veterans realise how difficult and unpredictable the markets can be. Ironically, just at the time more UK retail investors were getting involved in the stock market, two legendary investors, George Soros and Julian Robertson, were scaling back their activities. The two hedge fund managers, with decades of experience behind them, found that markets were too volatile and irrational.

But the private investors were ready to laugh in the face of irrationality. 'Once online, investors have access to vast quantities of investment data; these data can foster an illusion of knowledge, which increases overconfidence,' say Barber and Odean.[9] 'Online investors generally manage their own stock portfolios and execute trades at the click of a mouse; this fosters an illusion of control, which reinforces overconfidence.'

Charting

Frequent trading is often linked to 'charting' or 'technical analysis' as it is known. This is a school of thought that believes past patterns of share price movements can be used to predict the future. Its adherents follow rules as arcane as any mystical religion, and believe in them with a similar passion. Some draw patterns known as Japanese candlesticks. Others calculate moving averages of prices over twenty, fifty or 200 days.

To the outsider, such folks can appear completely mad. Take the enthusiasm for Fibonacci numbers, a sequence widely observed in nature. The Fibonacci series is constructed by adding the last two terms of a series to provide the next – thus 0, 1, 1, 2, 3, 5, 8, 13, 21 and so on. Mathematicians have shown this series has a strange property – over time, each number tends to be 61.8 per cent larger than its predecessor and only 61.8 per cent of its successor.

It's the kind of stuff that fascinates numerologists. But what potential relevance can it have to the stock market? Fibonacci enthusiasts argue a share price fall will often come to an end when the price has dropped to 61.8 per cent of its former level and a rally will end when the price has risen 61.8 per cent.

If you think that's bizarre, then how about Elliott wave theory? This holds that share prices always move in a succession of waves – an up phase (three up waves and two down) and a down phase (two down and one up). Having gazed at some of these charts myself, it can be pretty hard to tell whether you are supposed to be in the second down wave of an up phase or the first down wave of a down phase. Nevertheless, there are plenty of people prepared to believe in such theories and to pay good money for training sessions, books or computer programs which explain the mysteries of charts.

The key to all these schools of thought is that they can generate an awful lot of buy and sell signals. The private investor stares at the charts on his computer screen and spots patterns the way that fortune-tellers read life histories in the tea-leaves. The shares go up – buy; the shares go down – sell. The trading costs mount.

Investment clubs

Investment clubs are one of the hottest new ways for people to put money into shares. A group of people agree to invest a certain amount each month; they then meet once a month or so to decide which shares to buy. Each person might suggest a share, or one member a month might be asked to prepare a presentation on a particular stock.

The club format takes advantage of mankind's natural sociability. Each meeting is a social event, which makes investment more fun. The group approach allows each member to learn about the stock market in a relaxed atmosphere. Collective decision-making makes each club member feel more confident about the share buying process. And the kitty system means that a stock-picking failure should not do too much damage to each member's wealth.

In the US, the best-known club is probably the Beardstown Ladies, a group of elderly women who published a book detailing their investment successes and their favourite recipes. As it turned out, when the investment calculations were checked, their success was extremely exaggerated – they had significantly underperformed the market. But they inspired others to set up their own clubs (and sold a lot of books).

In the UK, ProShare has been promoting the investment club concept since 1996. 'Three years ago, there were 300,' says Jeremy King. 'In 2000, there were 9,000, and the total has doubled in twelve months.' All told, 130,000 people are involved in the investment club movement. Interest in clubs has clearly been fuelled by the stock market's performance, says King, and by the fact that people are increasingly aware that they can't rely on the state for retirement income. 'Lots of people don't want to learn about investment in an academic fashion and an investment club gives them a means of practical hands-on experience.'

ProShare provides clubs with starter packs, helping them with details such as club rules, dealing with brokers and handling club finances. Some have done remarkably well out of the recent stock market run. The top performing investment club in 1998 earned around 80 per cent, the top performer of 1999 achieved a return of 2,400 per cent.

It all seems pretty benign, and mostly it is. As long as investment club members do not expect too much in the way of a return. For reasons I discuss later in the chapter, I was rather alarmed to hear Jeremy King say that clubs should aim for a return of 14 per cent a year – that is way too high.

Enthusiasts for clubs say that they are not restricted in the same way that professionals are, so they can earn a higher return. Well, it is certainly true that investment clubs will have much more focused portfolios than a professional fund manager, perhaps half a dozen instead of fifty. That means their portfolios will be much more volatile than a more diversified return. So yes, some clubs may earn a lot more than the average fund manager; but equally some may earn a lot less.

A study by Brad Barber and Terrance Odean of the University of California in Davis studied the performance of 166 US investment clubs between February 1991 and January 1997. They found that the clubs underperformed the S&P 500 index, the main indicator for the US market, by an average of 3.9 percentage points a year.

Of the clubs studied, 60 per cent underperformed the market. Clubs also underperformed individual investors by about 2 percentage points a year. And the decision-making process was not very efficient: the shares the clubs bought subsequently earned lower returns than the stocks they sold.[10] The reason for the underperformance was that the clubs tended to focus on riskier stocks, to trade frequently and to own small amounts of several stocks, increasing the proportionate cost of trading.

So the evidence is that joining a club might be educational and fun, but it will not make you rich.

The savings game

You might think, with all this interest in equities, that Britons were piling up their savings in the late 1990s. Nothing could be further from the truth. The savings ratio dropped to a thirty-seven-year low in the second quarter of 2000, around 3 per cent of GDP.

One of the reasons for this is that the savings ratio is a net figure; it is the difference between income and spending. Consumers can, in theory, spend more than their income, since they can finance consumption through borrowing. And spending has been strong in recent years thanks to economic growth and rising employment.[11]

So a number of things have probably been happening. Some consumers have been squirrelling a large part of their income into unit trusts and in-dividual shares. Retail inflows to unit trusts have increased from an annual total of less than £4bn in 1996 to almost £18bn in 2000. The latter figure was equivalent to around 2 per cent of GDP. Others have been splurging on their credit cards. A third group has been doing both, reasoning, no doubt, that with the equity market pushing up the value of their savings, they can afford to buy a new car or take a holiday to the Caribbean.

In addition, those people who are saving are putting a bigger proportion of their holdings into equities. The building society has ceased to seem an attractive home for savings, especially for those who can recall late-1980s interest rates of 15 per cent. In the late 1990s, the best that investors could hope for was 6–7 per cent.

This fall in rates is more apparent than real. When investors were earn-ing 15 per cent, inflation was 10 per cent, so the real value of their money was eroding fast. With inflation at 2.5 per cent, a nominal return of 6–7 per cent is pretty good in historical terms. But when you compare it with the double-digit returns investors could have got from equities in the late 1990s, it does not seem that good. My mini-poll of *FT* readers found that most had switched from the building society into equities in search of better returns.

Long-term investment

Those *FT* readers were right as long as they were prepared to be patient. The figures are incontrovertible – if you're willing to invest for the long term, the best vehicle for your savings is the stock market.

According to Barclays Capital, if you put £100 into shares in 1945, and you reinvested all the income free of tax (admittedly an impossibility for the private investor), you would have had £103,120 by the end of 1999. Had you put the same sum into gilts (government bonds), it would have grown into just £3,018; in cash deposits, the £100 would have grown into £3,921.

That's a huge difference. And it's even starker if you allow for inflation. The real value of your initial investment in equities would have grown forty-five times over the fifty-four-year period. The real value of your cash deposit would have grown by just 72 per cent.

This outperformance is pretty uniform. Anyone who invested in equities during the twentieth century would have seen their portfolio beat cash in 68 per cent of all two-year periods, 77 per cent of five-year periods and 92 per cent of ten-year periods. But one should note that the figures from Barclays Capital are based on market indices, rather than actual performances. The indices do not allow for trading costs or tax – as a consequence, over the long term, the average investor will underperform any given index. The gap between the returns from share ownership and those from cash deposits will not be as large as the Barclays figures suggest.

Nevertheless, the lesson that equities are always the best investment has been drummed into private investors, particularly in the US. Any market setback, such as the sharp fall share prices suffered in the autumn of 1998, is seen as an opportunity to 'buy on the dips'. Even the crash of 1987, when shares in the US fell 22 per cent on one day – Black Monday – doesn't seem to put them off. After all, over the course of 1987 as a whole, the stock market was up.

The 'buy on the dips' approach has been supported by the actions of the US central bank, the Federal Reserve. When the market crashed in 1987, the Fed cut interest rates and helped stabilise the market. When it slumped in

1998, the Fed cut rates three times in a few weeks and share prices surged. Investors perceive that, whenever there is a market crisis, the Fed will ride to the rescue.

Investors in the UK seem to be adopting the same philosophy. And that is hardly surprising. Between 1977 and the time the internet mania took hold in the UK in late 1999, the stock market had just two down years – 1990 and 1994. In each of the calendar years 1995 to 1999, the market's annual percentage gains were in double digits. No wonder people thought that investing in the stock market was easy money; no wonder they had high expectations for future returns.

This view certainly seemed to be widespread among the *FT* readers I polled. Joe Cittern said, 'When the market corrects, often the good go down with the bad but the good recover whilst the bad (in this case, many of the frothy dotcoms) won't. If you have the cash or margin, the conviction and the nerve, that is an opportunity.' James McCarthy said, 'I think the markets will continue to be a place for long-term investment. Market over-reactions will allow the small investor to pick up some solid bargains if he or she is just prepared to wait.'

This stoicism can be quite sensible. If you are a long-term investor, then the worst thing you can do is panic when share prices are falling – all you will incur are extra trading costs. As one *FT* reader e-mailed me: 'It's important not to get carried away with euphoria or depression with short-term prices.'

But this attitude can breed complacency. As with all statistics, you can present the numbers in a different way. There have been several quite lengthy periods over the century when equity investors were staring at losses. According to the Barclays Capital figures, anyone who bought shares in 1909 would have had to wait till 1919 to make money. The same was true of 1928–35, 1936–46, 1946–54, and 1972–8. In real (after inflation) terms, share prices peaked in 1968 and did not regain those heights until 1993.

It is all very well knowing that equities will pay off over the very long term. But how long are most people's investment horizons? It can be very hard to persuade people to get interested in pensions until they are over forty. And even the best-laid savings plans can be disrupted by illness, or marriage, or unemployment, or childbirth.

In any case, it can be very hard for investors to hold on to their long-term principles when share prices are falling rapidly. In 1973–4, for example, the era of the oil crisis, rapid inflation, the miners' strike and the three-day week, shares fell 31.4 per cent and 55.3 per cent in successive years. One would have needed a strong nerve not to sell in those circumstances.

The worst type of bear market is one in which there is no climactic crash – giving an obvious buy signal – but a steady, remorseless decline. Every time investors buy on the dips, they find that they are worse off two months later. Each rally gives grateful investors the chance to sell their holdings and cut their losses.

Just take a look at the Japanese market. In late 1989, the Nikkei 225 Average peaked at just below 39,000. It then slumped and throughout the 1990s it never got close to that level again. Even in April 2001, the Nikkei was only a third of its peak level.

There are striking similarities with the US market. Analysts argued that traditional stock market measures such as the price–earnings ratio were irrelevant. Japanese companies were cited as examples for the rest of the world because of their emphasis on market share, not profit.

In the 1990s, the consensus shifted 180 degrees. Suddenly, Japanese managers were idiots, not idols. With shareholders imposing no discipline on their actions, they had invested in unprofitable projects and propped up lame duck subsidiaries. The results were disastrous and the Japanese spent the 1990s fighting off recession and deflation, with their financial sector in crisis.

The problem of low returns

It is both ironic and, in a way, inevitable that more people are becoming involved in the stock market at the very time that it is likely that returns will fall. All the evidence suggests it will be more difficult, not more easy, to earn high returns from this point in the market. Nominal returns will certainly be lower. In an era of 2.5 per cent inflation, double-digit annual investment returns will be extremely rare. But investors have yet to accept this.

This is, in part, due to that old problem of extrapolation. Returns from investments such as bonds and equities were very high in the 1990s, even though inflation was low for much of the period. It is natural to think such returns must continue – natural, but wrong.

To understand this point, you have to get the hang of a confusing concept called the yield. Let us start with the idea of interest on a building society account. If you have £1,000 in such an account and the building society pays you £100 a year, most people could work out that the interest rate is 10 per cent. The technical formula for this is to divide the interest payment (the £100) by the principal (£1,000) and multiply the result by 100. It works out at 0.1 times 100 or 10.

Roughly the same formula applies to the yield on an instrument like a bond or a share. The top line of the formula is the interest (on a bond) or the dividend (on a share). The key difference is the bottom line. Unlike a building society account, a share or bond is tradable. So, rather than compare the income with the amount you invested, you use the market value of your investment.

Confused? Suppose you invested £1,000 in a share that paid a dividend of £50 a year. The initial yield would be 5 per cent. But assume the share price doubles. You still get £50 a year in dividends, but your investment is now worth £2,000. Your yield is now 2.5 per cent. If the share price had halved, you would be getting a dividend of £50 on an investment worth £500. Your yield would be 10 per cent.

So the key concept here is that as a share or bond price rises, the yield falls, and as the price falls, the yield rises. Price and yield are what is known in the jargon as inversely correlated. This often causes confusion. A good day for bonds and shares is when prices rise, and therefore yields fall – that is not the case with a building society account, where there is no capital growth and any fall in the income return is bad news for the investor.

Having grasped the concept of yield, we need to move on to why prices rose and yields fell in the 1990s. For all of the 1970s and part of the 1980s, governments and central banks were grappling with the problem of high inflation. Inflation erodes the real value of money invested. Say you had £1,000 in a ten-year bond and the only product you could purchase was bread at £1 a loaf. Your original investment could buy you 1,000 loaves.

Over the ten years you owned the bond, prices rose at 7 per cent a year. That prompted the price of bread to double to £2 a loaf. But the value of your bond remained at £1,000. When you got your money back, you could buy not 1,000 loaves, but 500. The real value of your money had halved.

So, for obvious reasons, inflation is very bad news for bond investors. When inflation rises, therefore, they tend to sell bonds. And when the price falls, since the interest payment stays the same, the yield rises. Another way of looking at the subject is to say that bond buyers demand a higher yield to compensate them for the erosion of their capital.

The key is the *real yield*, the difference between the nominal yield and the inflation rate. If inflation is 2 per cent, investors might be happy with a nominal yield of 5 per cent, equivalent to a real yield of 3 per cent. If inflation rises to 5 per cent, the nominal yield will have to rise to 8 per cent to give investors a constant real yield of 3 per cent.

Shares are not so badly hit by inflation as bonds. This is because the value of shares is not fixed in nominal terms. When prices rises, so will the revenues of the corporate sector (because it produces the goods and services which are rising in price). Provided profit margins stay the same, profits will also rise when inflation rises. But dividend yields do tend to be higher when inflation is higher. This is partly because income-seeking investors demand a higher return; partly because shares compete with bonds for investors' wallets and, as bond yields rise, dividend yields tend to rise in tandem.

At the start of the 1990s, inflation was 10 per cent, shares were yielding 5 per cent and bonds 12 per cent. Britain was in the Exchange Rate Mechanism and struggling to defend the level of the pound; base rates were 15 per cent. Then, as the 1990s went on, slowly (miraculously for anyone who remembered the 1970s) inflation subsided. Britain gave up defending the pound, dropped out of the ERM and cut the level of base rates sharply. By the mid 1990s, inflation was as low as it had been for thirty years.

With inflation low, investors did not need to receive the high nominal bond and dividend yields they had demanded before. As yields fell, prices rose (thanks to our friend, inverse correlation). So investors enjoyed a decade of fantastic capital returns at a time of low inflation. It became easy to imagine that the good days would last for ever.

But it doesn't take a lot of thought to realise that a large part of those returns was a one-off. When the yield on shares falls from 5 per cent to 2.5 per cent, prices double. To get the same effect again, you have to cause the yield to drop to 1.25 per cent. But unless inflation is zero, that would mean investors would hardly be getting a real yield at all.

So how do we decide the future level of returns? Fortunately, part of the job of the actuarial profession is to work out the most likely level of investment returns over the long term. Actuaries have never had a great press; they spend a lot of time working out when people are going to die so that insurance companies can make a profit. But actuaries are skilled mathematicians and, unlike most of the people who work in the financial industry, they have no intrinsic interest in promoting higher share prices. So it is worth thinking about their logic.

They reason that the total return from equities in future will equal the dividend yield plus the annual growth in dividend payments. This may seem odd, especially in an era when dividends are seen as unimportant – many companies do not pay dividends at all. (Microsoft, the software company, has never paid a dividend but has made fortunes for any investor who backed it in its early days.) But at the aggregate market level, their reasoning is sound. Supposing you bought a tracker fund that mimicked the movements of the FTSE All-Share index. The dividend yield is 2.5 per cent, so for every £1,000 you invest, you get £25 a year in dividends. If there is no capital gain at all, you would make just £25 a year from your investment.

But remember that dividends can grow. If we assume that the dividend yield stays the same, then the growth in your investment must come from the growth in dividends. Say the dividend grows 8 per cent to £27 a year. At a constant yield of 2.5 per cent, your capital sum will grow to £1,080. Your profit will be £105 or 10.5 per cent – or the original dividend yield of 2.5 per cent plus growth of 8 per cent.

At the time of writing, the yield on the market is around 2.25 per cent. How much can we assume that dividends will grow? The standard actuarial assumption is to suggest that dividends will grow in line with corporate profits and profits will grow in line with the UK economy. The long-term average for UK economic growth is around 2.25 per cent. So that gets us to 4.5 per cent. Sounds a bit low? Of course, we've forgotten inflation. So let's assume that the Bank of England meets its inflation target over the long term. That means we can add in another 2.5 per cent.

Add that lot up and we reach a total of 7 per cent. The likely nominal return from equities, from current market levels, is 7 per cent. I'm going to guess that's rather less than most readers were expecting. From the mini-poll I conducted, I'm confident it's less than most private investors are expecting. And that 7 per cent is before any dealing costs or tax; 6 per cent might be a more realistic assumption.

Now you might easily think that this is one of those standard equations dreamt up by economists that make no sense in the real world. Let us try and challenge the model. Why on earth should the dividend yield stay constant at 2.25 per cent? Well, of course, it probably won't. The dividend yield has varied between 2.25 and 12 per cent in the course of the last thirty years, with an average somewhere in the 4–5 per cent range.

But actually the actuaries are being quite generous. Dividend yields are currently at the very low end of the historic range. A betting man would say they are more likely to rise than fall; that would cut returns to investors (remember that a rising yield means lower share prices).

Another objection might be that corporate profits could rise much faster than the rate of economic growth. They certainly have had periods of doing so in the past. The difficulty with this theory is that if corporate profits are rising more quickly than the economy, something else must be rising more slowly. In this case, the only possibility is wages.

Now there have indeed been short periods in which profits have risen faster than wages. But the suggestion, at the time of writing in late 2000, that such a trend is on its way looks rather odd. Unemployment in the US and the UK is at a twenty-five-year low. Employers are desperately seeking to hire, and hang on to, skilled staff. This is the stage of the cycle where wages gain at the expense of profits, not the other way round.

A report by the investment bank Goldman Sachs[12] concluded that the profits share of GDP was unlikely to rise on a sustainable basis. Over history, the share of GDP going to capital has been very stable at around one-third, with an average of 35.8 per cent. Labour's share of GDP has averaged 64.2 per cent and has fluctuated, on average, by only 1.7 points a year.

What about the internet? Couldn't it improve corporate profits? Goldman Sachs is doubtful. 'Suppose the internet means a particular firm can save £1m a year on its costs, perhaps by allowing a reduction in stocks of inventories. Will its profits also increase by £1m a year, indefinitely? No, at least, not if past experience is anything to go by. If one firm can save money on its inventories using the internet, then so can its competitors. The benefits tend to get competed away, as far as the corporate sector is concerned, and end up in the hands of consumers.'

As a breed, analysts tend to be pretty optimistic about future profit growth. IBES, a firm that compiles profit forecasts, said in 2000 that analysts were expecting long-term growth in US earnings of 17 per cent, a lot more than my assumption. But IBES also pointed out that, over the previous twenty years, analysts had been predicting an average of 17.6 per cent growth in earnings every year – the actual nominal growth rate was 7.8 per cent a year. (This latter figure is quite close to my assumption, given that inflation was higher in the 1980s than it is likely to be over the next few years.)

Given that profit growth was in single digits, how come the returns from investing were so high? The answer is that the return to investors comes in two ways. First, there is profit growth; second, there is the rating that investors are willing to apply to those profits.[13] This figure, known as the price–earnings ratio, rose sharply over the 1980s and 1990s and by early 2000 was close to a historic high.

What else could make our prediction look too pessimistic? Another possibility could be that GDP rises faster than the forecast, but it would have to rise a lot faster to make much of a difference. A 3 per cent growth rate assumption would only take returns up to 7.75 per cent.

Another possibility would be that inflation turns out to be higher than our assumption. But this would probably drive returns down, not up. As our previous reasoning has shown, if inflation was, say, 5 per cent, investors would demand a higher yield from shares. And a higher yield means lower prices.

Equity risk premium

You can reach the same sort of numbers if you approach the calculation from a different direction. Shares have traditionally produced better returns than either bonds or cash. This is due to the old principle that greater risk demands greater reward. If you keep your money in the bank, it will be safe, but it will not grow very much. To earn a bit more you have to take some risk. Shares are riskier than either bonds or cash.

The extra return that investors get from owning shares is known as the *equity risk premium*. If the return from owning shares is 8 per cent and the return from owning bonds is 5 per cent, then the premium is 3 per cent. The higher the premium, then the higher the risk of owning shares is perceived to be. Over the twentieth century, Professors Dimson and Marsh of the London Business School have calculated that the average premium was a little over 4 per cent.

The equation for calculating the equity risk premium is as follows – the dividend yield plus dividend growth is equal to the risk-free rate (the government bond yield) plus the risk premium. At the time of writing, the government bond yield was around 5.5 per cent. Add in the average risk premium for the last hundred years and you get 9.5 per cent.

What about the other side of the equation? As I said earlier, dividends are likely to grow at around 5 per cent a year. That would require the market to be on a yield of 4.5 per cent for the equation to balance. Since yields and prices are inversely correlated, that in turn would require the FTSE 100 to fall by around half from its late-2000 level.

But this seems a bit drastic. Equities are lot less risky than they used to be, because these days investors can create a diversified portfolio of shares and because the economy is more stable (less prone to recession). The risk premium can be a lot lower than it used to be. However, if the risk premium is a lot lower, that means *the excess returns from equities will be lower too.* Say the premium is 2 per cent. Add that to the current bond yield and you get a likely equity return of 7.5 per cent.

Thus, you can wiggle all you like but the most likely scenario is that returns from shares will be around 7 per cent in nominal terms. And if that reasoning is correct, it will be much harder to grow your savings quickly. There's an old maths rule called the rule of 72, which gives you a short cut to working out growth rates. You divide 72 by your assumed growth rate – that gives you the number of years for your investment capital to double. Had the growth rate been 14 per cent, it would have taken only five years to double. So £1,000 invested at 7 per cent would take about ten years to double to £2,000.

The good news is that inflation is lower. If you were aiming to accumulate a sum to bring you a decent income on retirement, that sum will be lower, in nominal terms, if inflation continues at 2–3 per cent, than it would have done under the 1970s and 1980s high-inflation era.

But as we saw earlier in the chapter, investor expectations tend to be much higher than that. They assume the returns achieved over the last twenty years will continue into the distant future. Even some professionals take the same view. One investor told me 'I have an investment planning manager and he tells me that with my investor profile, attitude to risk that I should expect a real return of 9 per cent and I guess I should believe him.' That kind of real return is well above the historical average, so the investment planning manager was either ignorant or unbelievably optimistic.

Endowment policies

The prospect of low future returns has created a particular problem for endowment policies. These are long-term insurance contracts, normally taken out with the aim of repaying a mortgage. The investor would put in a sum each month, part of which would be invested (normally in shares, bonds and property), part would be used to provide life insurance so that the mortgage could be paid off in the event of the policyholder's death and part would be put towards the insurance company's costs.

As it became clear in the late 1990s that inflation had fallen, the assumptions behind these policies started to crumble. Policies taken out in the late 1980s and early 1990s had been built on the assumption that high nominal returns would allow the policy to meet the cost of repaying a nominal sum (the mortgage). But alas, while nominal returns were set to fall in future, the amount needed to repay the mortgage would not decline. Some policies were set to fall short.

This issue, perhaps understandably, became confused with the issue of whether endowment policies had been mis-sold. Traditionally, endowments have been sold by people who earn commission on each policy. (The argument in favour of this system is that people rarely go out and buy life insurance of their own accord. They prefer not to think about their own death. These policies accordingly have to be sold; they are not bought.) But salesmen motivated by commission have an innate conflict of interest; is the sale of that policy good for the client or simply good for the salesman's bank account? It did not help that investors often did not realise they were paying commission and that the friendly person behind the building society or bank counter might have an ulterior motive for their advocacy of endowments.

This might not have been a problem were endowments more flexible. But they are built to reward long-term investors, usually over ten to twenty-five years. Those investors who cash out early have to face the full costs of the policy (including the salesman's commission); in the early years, that would mean getting less than their money back.

There are a lot of Britons who have neither the patience nor the ability (thanks to unemployment, sickness or divorce) to keep up payments for twenty-five years. One calculation found that almost a quarter of policies were abandoned in the first two years. Given that human trait, endowment policies should not have been sold as widely as they were.

But even if there had been no mis-selling, endowment policies would still have run into difficulties in a period of low nominal returns.

Real returns

To add to the problems facing investors, there is a case that real (after inflation) as well as nominal returns will be lower in the future. This is not a subject on which everyone would agree, but real returns have been much higher than the long-term average in recent years. (This has, of course, served to draw more people into the stock market. And, in a virtuous circle, as more investors are persuaded to invest in equities, share prices are pushed even higher.)

In the past, the stock market has shown a marked tendency to 'revert to the mean' – to follow a period of above average returns with a period of below-average numbers. The boom years of the 1920s were followed by the disastrous years of the 1930s. The go-go market of the 1960s was followed by the bear market of the 1970s. Some people, indeed, think that a 6–7 per cent nominal future return is far too optimistic. They point out that the stock market is trading at historically high valuations in terms of its profits and dividends. Share prices will have to fall sharply, rather than simply make slow progress, for the market to return to average valuations.

Two of the most prominent commentators to take this line are Andrew Smithers and Stephen Wright, whose book *Valuing Wall Street*[14] argued that the US stock market may be overvalued by as much as 60 per cent.[15] The Smithers-Wright thesis is that the value of the stock market and the replacement cost of the corporate sector's tangible assets should not get too far out of line. This relationship is known as the q ratio and was developed by the economist James Tobin. If the ratio is very high (as it was in 1998 and 1999), it is far cheaper to buy assets directly than to buy companies on the stock market in order to get hold of those assets. The market is overvalued. If the q ratio is below 1, it is cheaper to buy stock market companies in order to get hold of assets than to buy assets directly; the market is cheap.

Logic suggests that the two values should move back into line as they did in the late 1920s and late 1960s. If the stock market trades at a value far greater than its underlying assets, then logic suggests that the corporate sector must be earning a very high return on those assets. And if they are earning a very high return on their capital, then it makes sense for companies to invest more in the hope of further profits. Gradually, the greater amount of capital in use will increase competition and force down returns.

This does seem to be happening. According to investment advisers, Lombard Street Research, in 2000 'US business investment reached a share of GDP [14 per cent] last seen at the time of the twin recessions of the early 1980s. Its 1990s growth rate has only been paralleled, since the Second World War, in the mid-to-late 1960s. As then, the spur was a major initial upswing in the return on capital; as then the later stages of the business boom (1998–2000) have been accompanied by falling returns on capital, despite lower demand.'

Smithers and Wright also argue that recent US returns have been completely out of the ordinary. After analysing US stock market returns up for 200 years, they found that the returns achieved over the fifteen-, twenty-, and twenty-five-year periods till the end of 1999 had never been surpassed over the past 200 years.

Critics argue that Smithers and Wright are hopelessly outdated. In the new economy, tangible assets such as machinery and buildings have become far less important; what really matter are intangible assets, such as brand names and intellectual capital. Microsoft has hardly any physical assets at all but it is undeniably a very valuable company.

The argument quickly gets bogged down in economic terminology; Smithers and Wright argue, for example, that if the new economy thesis were true there would be signs that companies were using less capital than before. This is not the case. They also contend that the new economy thesis might be true if companies could be seen to be earning monopoly profits; in other words, if the corporate sector had become less competitive than before. In practice, however, the economy appears to be getting more competitive, not less.

It seems to me that critics dismiss Smithers and Wright rather too easily. Of course, it is right to say that intangible assets are more important these days than steel mills or machine tools. But what do intangible assets usually amount to? The brainpower of people. And given that you can't own people (they can always walk away from their jobs), the laws of economics will mean that eventually people who are creating wealth will expect more and more for their services. That will erode any increase in the return on capital.

This is a point that we can examine in more depth in Chapter 5, which deals with share options. But think about football for the moment. That is a business that depends entirely on the players. As a consequence, only a few clubs make a profit since the players demand ever-increasing wages. The clubs cannot turn down their demands, since the players can easily move elsewhere. Software programmers and website designers may be the football stars of the new economy.

Smithers and Wright are not the only people who think the market is overvalued. In his book *Irrational Exuberance*,[16] Robert Shiller, a Yale professor, argued that a number of factors had prompted shares to reach unsustainably high levels. There was much talk of a new era for the economy and the stock market in the 1920s, for example, but excessive investor optimism was crushed by the crash of 1929 and the depression of the 1930s.

'The present stock market displays the classic features of a *speculative bubble*: a situation in which temporarily high prices are sustained largely by investors' enthusiasm rather than by consistent estimation of real value,' wrote Shiller. 'Under these conditions, even though the market could possibly maintain or even substantially increase its price level, the outlook for the stock market into the next 10 or 20 years is likely to be rather poor – and perhaps even dangerous.' The views of Shiller, or Smithers & Wright, are not mainstream. There are plenty of people who think Shiller, like Smithers and Wright, is far too gloomy. In his book *Dow 100,000: Fact or Fiction*,[17] Charles Kadlec, managing director of J & W Seligman, decided that the prospect of the Dow hitting that large number by 2020 was more fact than fiction.[18]

Kadlec wrote that: 'Historical forces are aligned to produce a Great Prosperity – *at least two decades of above-average economic growth with price stability*. This will be a period of enormous business opportunities, rising living standards and a historic expansion in world commerce. Business and corporations will prosper by finding new and better ways to satisfy consumers. Real incomes will rise on a wave of productivity improvements brought about by technological advances. Radical reductions in the cost of communication will produce a global marketplace, if not a global village. The spread of freedom will bring with it extraordinary increases in prosperity in the developing world.'

If the FTSE 100 rose at Kadlec's target for the Dow – 11.1 per cent a year – then it would reach around 50,000 by 2020. If it grew by 5 per cent or so, as assumed earlier in the chapter, it would only reach 16,000: a vivid illustration of just how much difference compounding can make over a long period.

2

Tipping point

There are stories of people phoning brokers and saying 'I want to buy that share.' And the broker would ask 'Which share?' And they would say 'I don't know which one it was but it was on the telly.'

Industry expert

I n January 2000, shares in Coburg, a small coffee roasting company, suddenly doubled when an anonymous tipster posted a message on a financial website claiming the company was about to turn itself into an internet fund. Later in the day, the mystified company denied it had any such plans and the shares fell back to their original level. Tough luck if you bought at the top. But pretty good news if you bought before the rumour affected the shares and sold before the denial.

Pumping and dumping is what they call it in the trade. An investor, or a group of investors, assembles a significant position in a stock. They then spread a rumour that the company is about to win a new contract, get taken over, or (most recently) convert into an internet business. That causes the share price to soar and allows the conspirators to sell their shares and make a substantial profit. The victims of this scam are those who have been lured by the rumours into buying shares at a falsely high price.

Sometimes, the tactic is used the other way round. The conspirators spread malicious rumours about the company, with the aim of driving the price down. This is either because they have sold short (sold shares they

have borrowed in the hope of buying them back at a lower price) or because they would like to buy a significant stake in the company at a bargain
price.

In the US, there have been several instances of the pumping and dumping tactic. In April 1999, shares in Pairgain rose 30 per cent after a former
employee posted a false story on internet message boards, claiming the
company was poised to be acquired by an Israeli group. In August 2000, a
fake press release about a US company, Emulex, was circulated, causing the
shares to fall 61 per cent.

This is a tactic that can only work for certain types of shares. It would be
no use trying a 'pump and dump' operation on Vodafone, where daily
business runs into the hundreds of millions of pounds and the average investor is a clued-up institutional fund manager. This kind of scam works
only in the world of small company stocks, businesses valued at a few millions or tens of millions by the market, where not much business is trans-
acted each day, and where the main people trading are private investors. If
the professionals (institutions such as pension funds and insurance companies) are heavily involved in a particular share, one would expect them
either (a) to see through the ruse or (b) to ring the company or its broker
and check the story.

Nefarious tactics have been used in the stock market for centuries. In
the book *Confusion de Confusiones* (1688), Joseph de la Vega recounts the
scams undertaken in the seventeenth-century Dutch market. One successful ruse was to drop an apparently 'confidential' letter on the floor of the
market, giving negative or positive news about a company (depending on
whether the conspirators wanted to buy or sell). The beauty of this scam is
that it relied on the greed of other investors; their desire to trade on the
basis of 'inside information' was the cause of their downfall.

On Wall Street in the 1920s, the classic operation was the 'pool' in which
investors would heavily buy and sell a stock to give the impression of
pending activity. Naïve investors, those who indulged in an activity known
as 'watching the tape',[1] would be drawn into the fray as the price was drawn
higher. At just the right moment, the pool member would sell and the
share price would subside, leaving the tape watchers nursing a loss.

In the 1960s and early 1970s, similar activities were quite common. A
stockbroker or investor who wanted to sell his holding in an illiquid stock
would spread the rumour of a takeover, forcing the price higher. Hence
the old stock market saying 'a tip is a tap' – the person who is advising

everyone else to buy a particular share is usually taking the opportunity to sell.

The internet has merely created a new area of opportunity for those seeking to exploit the gullibility of others. Tips are still passed on in bars and by telephone (although the phone conversations of traders are now regularly taped by the banks that employ them). But the internet allows information to be passed speedily to large numbers of people via the message boards that appear on websites. And it also allows the tipsters to be anonymous in case the authorities start getting suspicious and try hunting them down.

There are plenty of eager recipients of what might be inside information. The breed of investor that emerged in late 1999, says Justin Urquhart Stewart of Barclays Stockbrokers, traded on 'rumour, hearsay and tittle-tattle. They weren't interested in things that went up 10–20 per cent, they were after a tenbagger [a stock that rises tenfold].'

There are vast numbers of financial websites in the US and the UK. Many give a combination of financial news, share price information, links to stockbrokers and message or bulletin boards, where investors can communicate with each other. The idea is that the investors will feel part of a 'community' and thus return to the site again and again. If a message board has tips, then so much the better; tips stimulate trading activity and the website will often have an arrangement with a stockbroker to share any commission income generated.

These bulletin boards can be highly influential. 'I remember an occasion on a Friday afternoon at 4.25,' says Nigel Reynolds, a director of stockbroker Charles Schwab (Europe). 'A customer wanted to buy 25,000 shares in a stock with a normal market size of 1,000 shares. So the marketmaker[2] bumped up the price from £6.10 to £7.50. We told the customer (about the vast price increase) but he had seen the shares tipped on a bulletin board and he still wanted them.'

It would be nice to think that these noticeboards are full of scholarly analyses of companies' prospects, allowing experienced investors to share knowledge rather like the research teams at an investment bank. Although some responses are intelligent, the average comment is mediocre stuff. Shares are tipped on the flimsiest of excuses.

Take three postings from the Interactive Investor International website in mid-August 2000. Author 'WLondon' says 'Buy Recall on Ofex [an exchange where shares in unquoted companies are traded]. Up 60 per cent since last week and still going … very large volumes … it's going to 50p by Friday and much more after that. Get while you can, this is a star.' Another author, 'Opprah', said 'Pile in Ofu. This will rocket to 4p.' And author, 'moonblue', said 'Last chance to buy IEH. One million quid buy (this morning) – 1 per cent of company value. Looks like a [sic] institution. Buy price will rocket when people wake up.'[3]

Note that in all three cases, the authors made no attempt to explain the company's business, let alone delve into its profits, assets or relation to the share price. These tips are based on the idea that the market is a casino and you might as well play your hunches.

All of the above messages are at least polite. On some days, the level of banter descends to that of an inner-city playground. Anyone who casts doubt on the chosen tip is a **** of some description. 'The bulletin boards have some very knowledgeable people and a few idiots,' says private investor John Delaney. The wise investors (and some of those on the bulletin boards do fall into this category) will ignore this kind of stuff altogether. After all, why should people sitting at their home computers possess the secret to investment success? And if they did, why would they pass it freely to others? Surely it would make sense to keep the information to themselves, buying as many shares as possible while they are still cheap. 'You've got to be cynical,' advises Richard Hunter, head of dealing services at NatWest Stockbrokers. 'If the professionals haven't heard of this stock, is it really a good story?'

The dangers of tipping

Readers sometimes e-mail me for 'hot tips' at the *FT*. My standard response is that we are not allowed, by law, to do so (this is not a cop-out. You have to be a registered financial adviser to give such recommendations.) But that's only part of the answer. A much more compelling reason for not giving tips is that *I don't know*. If I were so smart as to be able to pick winning shares, why would I be slogging in on the tube every day to an office on Southwark Bridge? I'd be relaxing on my yacht off the Bahamas.

This is the general problem with tipping, whether it is over the internet, in the press, on TV or face-to-face in the pub. Investors should always ask themselves: Why is this person telling me this? And why should I believe that he or she is right?

Jeremy King of ProShare says: 'We are very cautious about bulletin boards, particularly the concept of taking advice from someone you've never met and whose motives you know nothing about. At best, you should use the information as the starting point for research.'

Some message-board habitués might be genuinely altruistic. Many may well believe in the truth of the information they are passing on. But, of course, they won't make a profit unless enough people are made aware of the same information and act on it.

In some cases, the mere name of the tipster may be enough to move the share price. In the US, as recounted by John Emshwiler in his book *Scam Dogs and Mo-Mo Mamas*,[4] some of the tipsters with names like Tokyo Joe and Big Dog have developed large followings. Success in these cases can be self-fulfilling. If enough people believe in your investment acumen, then share prices will rise whether or not your tips are fundamentally sound. And the fact that they rise will be further proof of your expertise, which means your next tip will be even more successful, and so on.

Some investors might be jumping on the bandwagon for the very reason that it is a bandwagon. Never mind the fundamentals – if these people can genuinely move share prices, why not use them to make a profit? As an investment approach, it requires a lot less work than poring over balance sheets and reading the research notes penned by brokers.

There is, alas, a fatal flaw in this reasoning. Unless the information being touted is accurate (or unless, by luck, something else happens to validate a share price increase) then the share price will eventually revert to its original level. Any trading that goes on in the interim will be a zero sum game: as much money will be lost as will be won. Now who is more likely to be able to time their exit to perfection – the tipster who planted the rumour or the investor who followed the tip?

Old stock market hands have a term for this kind of investment – the 'greater fool' theory. The only reason for an investor to buy a share is to sell it to another investor – the greater fool – at a higher price. But at some point, the supply of greater fools will run out. And of course, to the person from whom you bought the share, *you* are the greater fool.

In principle, this is no different from the kind of pyramid scheme that occasionally becomes popular. You know the type of thing. You pay £5 to the person above you on the list and then recruit another two people to pay £5 to you. Everybody makes £5 on the list except of course the last people who get recruited. And since the world population (and particularly the gullible portion) is finite, that last line of recruits gets reached pretty quickly. Chances are by the time someone's bothered to recruit you, the pyramid is already about to topple.

So why do people believe these tips? In part, this must be because finance seems such a mystery – like a Masonic Lodge that you'll never be invited to join. It all seems so fearfully complicated that you will never understand it. Perhaps, just perhaps, the person giving the tip is one of those on the inside.

Certainly, years of covering the stock markets have taught me that people on the inside do know something. If a company is about to be taken over, its share price will generally start to rise before the deal leaks out. Someone in the know – the bankers, the lawyers, the executives, the accountants, or the public relations people – is buying the shares or passing the information on.

At the *FT*, we hear rumours of about five takeovers for every one that takes place. One can make some effort to check them out – but if you ring the companies concerned they will generally say 'no comment'. Brokers or bankers may give some 'off the record' guidance as to whether the rumoured deal is likely. But if the share price is rising sharply and lots of shares are being traded, that's a pretty good sign that *something* is going on. The authorities investigate these cases of insider dealing but it is usually very hard to prove – presumably the guilty men or women usually arrange for the dealing to be done by a friend who is willing to share the profits.

It used to be that this kind of insider dealing was not only legal, but commonplace. Financial journalists used to earn less than their mainstream colleagues because they were presumed to profit from tips. Nowadays, there are strict rules designed to prevent them from doing so (but see below). None the less, the general public still tends to think that the market is either rigged (in which case, they want to make friends with the riggers) or a lottery (in which case, they might as well speculate wildly).

The lottery thesis may be a bit more clever than it seems. In the 1950s and 1960s, academics started to believe that stock markets were 'efficient' – that is, prices already reflect all the available information. Trying to use publicly available information to pick shares is therefore pointless. Professional investors often scoff at efficient market theory[5] but in fact the laugh is on them. All the evidence suggests they fail to beat the stock market index – which represents the performance of the average investor. The

time they spend analysing company balance sheets, talking to managements and crunching numbers on their computers is effectively wasted.

To be fair to fund managers, the task of beating the market is a very difficult one. Professional fund managers own the bulk of the stock market
(in the UK, at least) and the index is designed to represent the performance of the average stock in the market. By definition, therefore, around
half the managers would expect to be below average. But the managers face
a further handicap in that the index does not allow for the costs of trading
or for fund managers' fees. So, on this basis, it is hardly surprising that
most managers fail to beat the index.

Still, it is striking how random performance appears to be. Research on
behalf of the Financial Services Authority (the UK's financial regulator)
has found that past performance is no guide to the future. Even if you pick
a manager who has beaten the index in the past, he or she is no more likely
to do so in future than someone who has underperformed.

So, yes, the market is a bit of a lottery. But the answer is not to treat it
like a gamble. If you despair of the task of picking stocks, I do have one tip
for you – the only one in the book. Forget stock picking – buy an index
fund, a unit trust designed to mimic the performance of the market. As
long as you buy a broadly spread index fund with low costs, you are virtually guaranteed to perform better than the average investor over the long
run.

My advice is far from original – you can get it from a lot of personal finance experts any day of the week. Alas, it's not a very exciting approach –
it doesn't persuade readers to buy your paper or magazine every week or
earn much commission for advisers who recommend it. And, as has already been mentioned, investors tend to be remarkably confident about
their ability to avoid the mistakes of others and pick the right stocks for the
long term. They will be smart enough to beat the index, if only they get the
right information. So they may not get share tips from the *Financial Times*
but they will seek them out elsewhere.

Penny shares

Often the companies that get tipped on bulletin boards have very low
share prices and are known as 'penny shares' in the jargon. The definition
of a penny share depends on whom you ask, but let us say it is a share trading for less than 50p.

The allure of a penny share is a source of great wonder but it clearly runs deep within many investors' minds. To them, a stock that trades at 10p is cheap whereas one that trades at £10 is expensive and that is all there is to it. Alas, this is complete nonsense from beginning to end. A share represents a share of a company's assets and profits. What matters is how much assets and profits each share represents; the actual share price tells you nothing without that additional information.

Say you were offered a choice of beer for £1 or beer for £10; which would be the better deal? It all depends, of course, on *how much* beer is being offered. If you are just getting a teaspoonful for £1, it is a bad deal; if you are getting five gallons for £10 it is a good one. The same applies to shares. A share in a worthless company is still expensive at a penny. A share might be cheap at a billion pounds if, for example, it represented a claim over £2bn of assets.

It seems very hard to convince people of this. Some people like to get 'more shares for their money' – if they invest £1,000 in a company, they would rather get 2,000 shares than 500. But this is still utter folly. Their maximum loss is the same either way – £1,000. To counter this irrationality, companies will often have a bonus or scrip issue if their share price gets to be more than £10 – handing out, for example, one free share for every one in existence. The value of the company is entirely unchanged by this process but the share price often goes up when a bonus issue is announced! Imagine a restaurant being able to charge more for its pizzas when sliced into eight instead of four.

It is true to say that small company shares have tended to outperform large company shares over the long run and it is also true that penny shares tend to be associated with smaller groups. But it is the fact that the companies are small, not the level of the share price, which is the key.

Penny stocks also tend to have greater dealing costs than the shares of established 'blue chip' companies such as British Telecom or Barclays Bank. This is because of the 'spread' – the difference between the buy and sell prices on such stocks. Say that you see in the paper that the share price of Acme Widgets is 2p. That figure merely represents the average of the buy and sell prices. If you wanted to trade, the spread might be 1.5–2.5p. In other words, if you wanted to buy you would have to pay 2.5p whereas if you wanted to sell you would only get 1.5p. *To make any profit at all, the sell price would have to rise to 2.75p, or over 80 per cent.*

Ah, but, the penny stock enthusiasts will claim, if a 2p stock goes to £20, then your £1,000 will turn you into a millionaire. The upside is almost infinite but the downside is only 2p. No, the downside is 100 per cent of your original investment whether you pay 2p or 200p.

The shell game

One variant of the penny stock phenomenon was revived in the 1999–2000 period – the art of the 'shell', a company whose main asset is not its business but its stock market quote.

There were shell companies around not long before the rise of the internet. And there will be shells long after the internet is old hat. The trick looks complicated but is really simple. Say Shellco is worth £1m and has 1m shares. Outsiders have a business called Realco worth £10m. The outsiders persuade Shellco to make a takeover offer for Realco, offering 10 million new Shellco shares. The owners of Realco accept. As a result, they now have 10m shares out of the 11 million issued by Shellco, and thus have control of the company. This process is known as a 'reverse takeover' because while it looks on the surface as if Shellco is making the purchase, in reality the owners of Realco are taking control. The combined business appears to be worth much more than the old shell, so the shares go up in price. That benefits the new majority shareholders.

In some cases, the shell does not actually acquire a new business but is simply 'occupied' by a new set of investors, who move in and buy a stake. Rather like the *Invasion of the Body Snatchers*, the outside of the company is unchanged but its personality has altered.

The new investors bring their famous names rather than an actual business to the table. If these people have been successful before, then they will attract a fan club of smaller investors who will back any deal they propose. Those investors will push up the share price; the shell will become the 'hot new thing' on the market. The company can then use its highly valued paper to buy a 'real' business and success is assured.

Well, that's the theory.

A fine example of the shell phenomenon was Blake's Clothing. This company was a struggling menswear retail company and became a shell when it sold its trading subsidiary Casanova Fashions, leaving it with £1.3m of net assets.

Hey presto! Throw in a change of name and strategy – to e-xentric, a company with plans to invest in e-commerce and web businesses. Throw in some names that might catch the fancy of investors – Edward Charles Albert Spencer-Churchill, son of the Duke of Marlborough, Hugh Osmond, chairman of the pubs group Punch Taverns and Charles Nasser, who had founded an internet service provider Claranet. Add in a capital raising exercise, with a share issue at 2.25p per share.

The resulting concoction was duly intoxicating. The shares, which had been suspended ahead of the deal, rose from 7.75 to 146.25p on their return. The company, with just £3m of assets, was now valued by the market at £220m.

Good news if you got in and out of the shares at the right time. One bulletin board correspondent claimed 'Blake's in and out in 20 minutes. Made 1k. I'm gonna have a good lunch.' Another investor, a Birmingham councillor, claimed to have made a profit of £500,000, having bought the shares before the suspension.

Of course, if you were caught up in the hype and bought at the end of the first day of trading, you might not be quite so pleased. By early April 2001, the shares had drifted back to 12p. Anyone who bought at the end of that first day had lost more than 90 per cent of their money.

The famous name approach was best exemplified by Knutsford, a shell company backed by Archie Norman (ex-head of Asda and a Conservative MP), property developers Nick Leslau and Nigel Wray and Julian Richer, a hi-fi retailer. When the foursome moved into the company, the shares rose from 9.25p to touch 252p within the first day of trading and there was talk of the group buying a big retailer like Storehouse or Marks & Spencer. The 'awesome foursome' and their management skills were about to transform Britain's high streets.

As so often, the initial promise petered out. Instead of bidding for a retailer, Knutsford made an approach to an industrial conglomerate called Wassall. There was widespread disappointment at the chosen target and although the shares were trading at 175p in the market, institutions refused to support a share issue at 30p to fund the deal. Norman then declared he would have to devote most of his energy to being a shadow cabinet spokesman.

Without Norman, the original plans to become a retail giant had to be abandoned. The company switched its focus to – what else? – online investment and was itself reversed into by a US financial information business, Wilink.com. The shares, which at one point reached 265p, were trading in April 2001 at 3.25p – a loss to those who bought at the peak of almost 99 per cent.

The creation of internet incubators provided a variant on the shell phenomenon. An incubator is a fund that, as well as investing in small companies, also gives them management support and other help (providing offices, for example). When they came to the market, they had nothing but money and good intentions. But from the point of view of small investors, they were seen as getting in on the 'ground floor' of the next internet greats.

Oxygen was one such incubator backed by names such as Elisabeth Murdoch, daughter of Rupert, her partner Matthew Freud, the PR man, and Michael Edelson, an entrepreneur behind a whole string of shells, including Knutsford. The idea behind the company was that it would back internet ideas dreamed up by students. The shares, floated at 2p, jumped to 65p on the first day of trading.

Why were the shares priced so highly? You cannot say it was because the company had made some great investments; *at the time of flotation, it had no investments.* Perhaps investors thought the fund would buy into internet start-ups at a bargain price. The flaw in that idea is that, at the time, funds were falling over themselves to invest in new internet businesses. The price of start-ups was being forced higher.

And the share price also presupposed an odd type of student entrepreneur – someone sufficiently brilliant to dream up a successful new business but sufficiently stupid to sell it to Oxygen for one-thirty-second of its true worth. Again, disappointment was the inevitable result. By early April 2001, the shares had slumped all the way back to 1.25p. A number of other stocks followed a similar path, such as Bizzbuild (peaked at 317.5p, slumped to 13.25p) or Legendary Investments (hit 20.75p, fell back to 1.5p).

Why did these share prices rise so much, on the basis of such flimsy evidence? One reason was undoubtedly the bandwagon effect – investors were told by friends, or sometimes by newspapers, that such shares would be 'sure things'. The lure of easy money proved more powerful than reason. 'I invested in Oxygen because of the hype – a bad decision on my part,' said one investor, Lesley McGuire. 'It then fell 80 per cent.'

New issues

Private investor enthusiasm for new issues (also known as initial public offerings, or IPOs) tends to be almost as great as that for penny stocks and shells. As with internet incubators, investors seem to feel they are getting in on the 'ground floor' of a great new stock.

But new issues also represent one of the most frustrating parts of the stock market for private investors. In most cases, they are excluded from the chance to buy the shares at the offering price – instead, the shares are placed with institutional investors. From the point of view of the company, this means that their shares are in the hands of the kind of big investors who can stump up the money to fund their future expansion plans.

From the point of view of the investment bank or broker who handles the issues, this system is a useful way of rewarding their best clients – by giving them big chunks of the hottest new issues. But from the point of view of private investors, it is nothing but bad news. They are forced to buy when dealings on the market begin. And if the issue is successful, that means they are forced to pay a higher price than the institutions. It is one price for the rich and one for the poor.

A survey by Old Mutual Securities shows just how bad a deal this is for private investors. They found that the average new issue in the 1990s went to a 28 per cent premium at the end of the first day of dealings. But from that point, the average new issue underperformed the rest of the market by 15 per cent over the next three years. No problem if you bought the shares at the offer price; very bad news if you bought at the end of the first day.

Nor are things necessarily any better when private investors *are* allowed to participate. They then face a Catch-22 situation. If the issue is a great success, so many investors will apply for shares that successful investors will get few shares each. If the issue is a flop, anyone who applies will get all the shares they want – but since the share price will probably flop after flotation, that will not seem a good deal.

The flotation of Lastminute.com was a case in point. Such was the hype surrounding this company that many investors expected it to be a great success. And by expecting it to be so, they made it so. Few could resist the lure of easy money. What many investors were aiming to do was to get as many shares as possible and sell them as quickly as possible, a process known as stagging.

'There were a whole lot of investors who thought that every IPO was a winner,' recalls Ross Greenwood, editor of *Shares* magazine. The initial price range for the Lastminute issue was 190–230p per share. But the spread betting firms (see Chapter 6), which speculate on the performance of new issues, were forecasting that the first day price could reach more than 500p. Not surprisingly, Morgan Stanley, the investment bank behind the offer, increased the price to 380p. That was no crime – it is the duty of the investment bank to raise the maximum possible total for their client.

Even with the price rise, the demand was overwhelming. Investors clamoured for forty times as many shares as were on offer. Instead of having a ballot – satisfying the total demand of a few investors, while disappointing the vast majority – Morgan Stanley spread the shares thinly. Private investors were allocated just thirty-five shares each, making their holding worth £133. Nobody was going to become a millionaire on the back of that size of holding.

As a result, there was widespread disillusionment. Although the shares briefly reached 560p on the first day, a lot of investors decided to move on and look for the next opportunity. To make matters worse, there was a sudden slump in Nasdaq, the US technology market. Lastminute shares quickly halved. By April 2001, the shares had slipped to 44.5p, making the holding of any successful applicant worth just £15.58. At that price, they were not worth selling; dealing costs would eat up the proceeds.

Investors often complain about this problem on bulletin boards. The *FT* readers I polled seemed philosophically resigned. Malwa Cotton attempted to lay his hands on IPOs before they shot up after listing. After six months, he described his experience as 'mixed. I have not lost much but have not gained either.' 'I stagged Interactive Investor but that's about it. Most new issues aren't available to the private investor,' said Martin Newton, a retired police officer who now trades from home.

Tips and the media

Giving the readers what they want – share tips – is the kind of journalism that can be very successful in the short term. The City Slickers column in the *Daily Mirror* appeared for a while to be enormously successful. It had a fresh irreverent style that was designed to appeal to a tabloid readership. Stocks were enthusiastically tipped with readers invited to 'fill their boots'. By and large, the shares that the authors tipped generally did substantially rise in value. Its top ten tips for 1999 produced returns of 142 per cent.

Not only were the authors easier to read than the type of financial journalism that appears in the *Daily Telegraph* or *Financial Times* but, for anyone looking for 'easy money', their columns were far more useful.

The *FT* doesn't really go in for tips, save for some freelance writers in the weekend section. The Lex column on the back page does opine that the odd share looks expensive or cheap, as do some of the writers of company comments. I myself have written about stock-picking systems that use investment criteria such as dividend yield to select a diversified portfolio of shares.

But nobody says: 'Fill your boots'. That is not because the writers are stuffy or lack the courage of their convictions. There are quite sensible legal reasons why those who give investment advice are supposed to belong to a regulatory body. Anybody who gives advice should need to be aware of a client's circumstances – the kind of investment that is suitable for a twenty-nine-year-old banker earning £100,000 a year would not meet the needs of an eighty-year-old widow on a small pension.

And how do writers get those share tips? Alas, as with most journalism, this doesn't depend on brilliant detective work in the manner of Hercule Poirot. Someone has to give you that information – and that someone will have their own motivation for the tip.

As the Press Complaints Commission described in its ruling on the Slickers:[6] 'In very broad terms, stories which appeared in the [City Slickers] column came from one of four main sources: the companies concerned (or at least individuals close to those companies); financial public relations agencies retained by companies to place media stories; brokers (either the brokers to the companies concerned or, more usually, brokers who had picked up market rumours relating to companies which they did not represent); and City analysts employed elsewhere in the financial press.'

It's fair to say that many of the people giving the information would have an interest in seeing good news in the press about the shares. Either they would own the shares themselves, or they would be representing the company concerned – and a higher share price would improve the company's ability to undertake transactions, such as takeovers, and thus increase the advisers' fees. So even though the journalists might have been passing on the tips with the best of intentions – to make the readers money – this was not exactly objective advice.

The other problem with share tipping is that it is a kind of drug. You want your shares to perform well, so therefore you slant your news stories to favour that company. If your judgement proves right, you start to feel that you too should reap the benefit of your share-dealing acumen. So you start to buy the shares you tip.

In the case of the City Slickers, this is exactly what happened. To return to the Press Commission judgment, 'It was in these circumstances that Mr Bhoyrul and Mr Hipwell began to purchase shares which were featured in the column. The Commission was told that on a number of days they identified a share that would become the next day's "tip of the day"; then purchased a number of shares; published the "tip of the day" and then sold the shares on the day of the tip. The Commission was told that Hipwell had supplied details which indicated that he had followed such a procedure on at least 25 occasions and Bhoyrul had specifically detailed doing so on at least six. The newspaper also stated that there were other occasions on which shares, which the two journalists owned, were featured in the City Slickers column.'

This is a distinct problem for financial journalism in the modern age. Journalists can hardly be objective reporters if they have a financial interest in the company concerned.

The Press Code of Conduct states that:

> *1. Even when the law does not prohibit it, journalists must not use for their own profit, financial information which they receive in advance of its general publication, nor should they pass such information to others.*
> *2. They must not write about shares or securities in whose performance they know that they or their close families have a significant financial interest, without disclosing their interest to the editor or financial editor.*
> *3. They must not buy or sell, either directly or through nominees or agents, shares or securities about which they have written recently or about which they intend to write in the near future.*

These rules do not prohibit journalists from owning shares at all. One argument is that if journalists cannot own shares, then they will miss out on the benefits of a rising equity market. But they do not have to own individual shares – writers can have holdings in unit or investment trusts (two types of collective funds). They will still receive the benefits of stock market investment, without creating any conflict of interest.[7]

A further defence of journalistic share ownership is that writers should 'put their money where their mouths are'. After all, if they are not prepared to buy the shares, why should a reader take any notice of their advice? Furthermore, by getting involved in the stock market, they gain knowledge and experience that they can pass on to readers. Certainly, 'diary of an investor' columns are usually very popular with readers. Usually, they are compiled by freelancers, rather than staff members. But this does not really get round the conflict of interest problem.

One simple answer is disclosure. *Shares* magazine lists four rules, plus a disclaimer, on its editorial page. The rules include the following: 'Reporters who intend to write about any securities, derivatives or positions with spread betting organisations that they have an interest in should first clear their writing with the editor or deputy editor. If the editors agree that the reporter can write about the interest, it should be disclosed to readers at the end of the story.'

Reporters are also not allowed to deal in shares they write about in the month before, or the month after, the article appears. This rule is designed to prevent the 'pumping and dumping' approach. Usually, a journalistic tip has only a short-term effect on a share price.

Furthermore, reporters are required to hold a full personal interest register, which is available to the editor. A register is not a foolproof system but it does create a presumption of guilt if it is discovered that he or she has been writing about, and trading in, shares that are not on the register.

A more intractable problem is that of family members. Although the Press Code of Conduct specifically refers to the family, the days of the Victorian *paterfamilias* are long gone. Modern spouses often have different names and may wish to keep their financial interests entirely separate from those of their partners. It is a rare person these days who would know the details of the financial affairs of a sibling or an uncle. But to exclude such people from the regulations would create a gaping loophole for the unscrupulous: tip the shares, get Uncle Sid to buy them and split the profits.

Of course, cheats will always get round these rules, no matter how carefully they are devised. But it is not only insiders who exploit the system.

Show Me the Money is a Channel 4 programme focused around investment. It is structured as a game show with teams of three people asked to pick stocks. During each show, the team members are presented with a 'top tip' by an outside expert and (in a somewhat undignified process) a '60-second pitch' by the chief executive of a listed company.

It is only 'a bit of fun' as TV executives tend to say; no real money is changing hands. But the structure of the show encourages all the wrong tendencies in investors. Teams are judged on a week-by-week basis – far too short a term to make a proper assessment of an equity portfolio. And neither the top tip, nor the 60-second pitch, gives investors anything like enough information to make a rational choice. On one show I saw in November 2000, a team of teenagers selected the top tip of the day although the expert's previous selection had fallen by 50 per cent.

It may be true that the presenters intone the traditional warnings about shares going down as well as up and that one of them, Tom Winnifrith, makes sound and cautionary points. But the general effect of the show is to encourage short-term speculation.

According to Jeremy King of ProShare: 'There are stories about people phoning brokers and saying "I want to buy that share." And the broker would ask "Which share?" And they would say "I don't know which one it was but it was on the telly."' Investor John Delaney says that during the first series of *Show Me the Money,* 'my broker would phone me during the show with his finger on the trading button. Some stocks I'd buy as soon as they were mentioned and sell half an hour later.'

'*Show Me the Money* encouraged a bit more of a gambling mentality. The marketmakers would watch the show as well. As soon as a stock was tipped, the share price would go up a few pence,' says Nigel Reynolds of Charles Schwab.

Indeed, they did more than that. In the early days of the show, the names of the companies that appeared were announced in advance. Surprise, surprise, they had a tendency to rise on the morning *before* the programme was shown. In September 1999, the producers of the show, Princess Productions, understandably decided to discontinue this process.

One should stress that there was absolutely nothing illegal in a marketmaker pushing up the price of a share before the show. For a start, the company's imminent appearance was publicly available information. Secondly, a marketmaker is not a charity. If a trader knows there is going to be increased demand for a particular share, he will push the price up. That is how a market works; supply and demand are balanced by price. Exactly the same effect can be seen on a Monday morning. Shares tipped in the financial pages of the Sunday newspapers will rise in price before private investors have a chance to take advantage of the tip.

But the nature of share tipping can create traps for the unwary. What could be healthier, for example, than an executive buying shares in his own company? In November 1999, one executive, Barry Moat, managing director of Premier Direct, a display marketing company, decided to unwind a share deal after he bought 8,000 shares in his company on the morning of his appearance on *Show Me the Money*. The shares duly shot up and Mr Moat would have been more than £6,000 ahead on the day had the deal stayed in place. Reversing the deal removed any suggestion of impropriety.

In the end, however you devise the rules, share tipping in the media or on the internet just throws up too many issues and creates too many potential conflicts of interest. Sensible investors should, in any case, ignore the tips; at the best they should be starting points for further analysis, at the worst, they are no more useful than the horoscopes.

Investment advice should really be tailored to an individual's needs. Some private investors need income, for example, so tech stocks that often pay no, or very low, dividends are unsuitable. Execution-only brokers are no help in this regard. Of course, it would be foolish to suggest that stockbrokers have a monopoly of wisdom. There are many examples of investors who have been given stupid advice by a broker. But a good broker should steer clients away from the most speculative stocks and ensure that they have a sensible spread of holdings.

As for journalists and TV executives, share tipping may be popular but sometimes you should be careful about giving the public what it wants.

3

The Net

The trouble with the internet is that it destroys margins,
thereby destroying service levels because it can only sell on price.

Small businessman

A glum-faced earthworm gazes at the camera, while a voiceover croons a song of lament. In the distance, two children happily play ball. The worm looks up in horror as a gardener's spade comes down towards it. Its body is cut in two. But then, the severed bottom half of the worm grows its own head. The two halves head a ball between each other while the song turns upbeat. A voiceover intones 'Life is great. See MSN.co.uk for details.'

For anyone without a computer, this advert on UK television was completely pointless. Even for people who did have a computer, what was the ad trying to say? What is MSN.co.uk? A website for gardeners? Or people with split personalities? Or people who like seeing animals injured? But that was the nature of early dotcom advertising. Never has so much money been spent on reaching so many, when so few could understand what the hell was going on.

It is a new industry, of course, and in a new industry, consumers have no idea of brand names. The first wave of advertising revenue is thus designed to get your name known. Once that is achieved, the detailed stuff can come later. Or so the theory goes.

The strategy has a perfectly respectable history. Remember the mobile phone ads that intoned 'The future's bright. The future's Orange.' A pretty meaningless set of words but a phrase that did stick in the memory. When consumers started shopping for mobile phones, Orange was a brand name they easily recognised.

The internet was, in effect, unconquered territory for businesses. In the early days, it was thought that the best approach was to get out there and plant as many flags as possible. Don't worry too much about profit. That would come later once the name was known and the business established as the number one in its sector. You might call this the 'shoot for the moon' approach.

Take Rob Golding, a former stock market analyst who joined a company called Tornado-Insider, which provides information on technology companies, at the height of the dotcom boom. 'The model was to give everything away and hope that, in due course, people will enjoy it and place a value on it. In year 1, build a brand, year 2, build a business and year 3, build the revenues.'

Building a business for the long term, without worrying about profit in the short term, does not seem a completely unreasonable idea. But the difficulty with the approach is that it can lead to a kind of closed logic. There is an old joke, which I first recall being performed by Laurel and Hardy. A bystander says: 'So what do you guys do?' Hardy says: 'We're elephant hunters.' 'But there aren't any elephants in New Jersey,' the bystander retorts. 'Exactly,' says Laurel, 'that just shows how good we are.'

Early internet strategy seemed to involve spending as much as possible. 'You're losing a fortune,' the casual observer might say to the folks in charge. 'Exactly,' would come the reply. 'That shows how well we're doing.' There was nothing, on the surface, to distinguish the good from the bad businesses – they were all losing money and were proud of it.

Another problem with the 'shoot for the moon' approach is that it is extremely risky. Boo.com was a fashion retailer that spent large sums on marketing in an attempt to establish a trendy image as part of its long-term strategy of selling clothing to young people over the net. It was a plausible target market. The net was perceived to be hip; young people are more likely to use the net; a significant proportion of their expenditure is on clothes.

Investors like the words 'young' and 'hip' perhaps because they are rarely young and hip themselves. When Boo.com did the rounds of the international investment companies, they were welcomed with open

chequebooks. According to Mick McLoughlin, a corporate recovery partner at KPMG who acted as liquidator of the company, he was told that 'they
did rounds of funding where they basically rang the investors up and said,
for instance "we're raising $30m on this round of funding, your share is five
million, you've got ten minutes to decide whether you're in or not", put the
phone down and wait for the phone to ring back, which we are told it did.'[1]

All told, the founders raised around $135m (£90m) from international
investors. Had you visited the same folks with an idea for an engineering
business or a plastics factory, you would have been shown the door. To the
liftshaft.

Of the money raised, McLoughlin reckons[2] the company spent, in just a
year, around $40m on staff, $25m on advertising and promotion, $20m on
consulting and IT investment, and $15m on sundries including legal and
office costs.

In May 2000, Boo became the first high profile UK dotcom company to
go bust. According to McLoughlin, 'I think they (the founders) got carried
away with the pioneering spirit of trying to do two things – one, trying to
build a global brand very quickly. And two, trying to build a very complex
technology platform to deliver that brand.'

When McLoughlin came to liquidate the company, he found there was
not that much to sell. 'If we split it into two, the bit that everybody knows
about is the website so you actually have the name in the main site – that
we did sell but we only had two offers and eventually sold it to an American company [called] fashionmail.inc. The technology platform that
everybody got excited about basically consisted of a bunch of electrons.
Boo didn't own their hardware – it was all leased and 95 per cent of the
software that they used was under licence from various software houses. So
it was basically a small piece of software and the knowledge in a few people's heads, that's all we had to sell.'

The two disposals together raised less than £1m. By the time it was liquidated it had sold just $1.5m worth of goods. So the dotcom Emperor not
only had no clothes, it could not sell them either.

The whole process of creating and folding Boo.com, like the Lottery, involved a transfer of wealth. Money was taken from investors and given to
staff, advertising agencies and technology consultants. Nobody got rich on
the deal (although they enjoyed a few lavish parties while the company
lasted). The investors simply paid a lot of money to learn one of the oldest
lessons in the book; the odds are against new companies succeeding.

And when it comes to liquidation, a new economy company is not like a manufacturing business, where there is usually machinery, stock and even property to sell. As McLoughlin says, 'The difficulties in dealing with dotcom companies are that they have little in the way of tangible assets, highly mobile staff and we were dealing with a very volatile market.' Shareholders and creditors are unlikely to receive much in the way of return from a dotcom failure.

He warns that, to ensure success, 'Companies need proper business plans, proper financing, strong management and a proper contingency plan if things go wrong.' Boo.com simply didn't have a contingency plan when initial sales didn't meet expectations.

Part of Boo.com's problem was that it aimed for a very ambitious technological platform that could be used by consumers with high-speed internet access. But most customers simply didn't have the ability to take advantage of this platform.

This was a problem facing all internet pioneers. UK internet access was initially slow, cumbersome and expensive for most people – much more so than it was in the US. In the US, local phone calls are free, allowing net users to stay on the line for ever. But in the UK, the local network is controlled by BT, which charges internet companies for providing a service. That led to big battles between BT and the telecoms regulator, Oftel, about opening up local lines so that competition could flourish.

An attempt by one US company, AltaVista, to launch an unlimited access service based on a flat fee collapsed amid much embarrassment. Although tens of thousands signed up the company was forced to admit that it was unable to offer the service because it could not make a profit. Only in late 2000 was the charging system of BT changed, enabling companies like America Online (AOL) to launch unmetered services on an economic basis.

Even those who have an internet link do not always find it reliable. All computer users know the feeling. You enter your password and wait to get through to the internet service provider. A series of high-pitched squeaks and piano chords ensue. If you're lucky, you get through first time; if not, the whole noisy process must be repeated. To find the site you want, you have to remember a complicated string of symbols that may well include colons, forward slashes and several full stops, not to mention some combination of http, www, com or co.uk. Enter the code and you may get instantly through or, for no apparent reason, the computer may seemingly go into a deep coma. You can make a cup of tea, read the paper, feed the cat and it will still be just sitting there.

And consumers who survive all this to try to make a transaction on the net can also be frustrated. Often a lengthy registration form needs to be filled in – something that does not happen when you enter a shop.

Even when you succeed in ordering goods, there can be a big gap between promise and delivery. A survey undertaken by the Trading Standards Institute in October 2000 found that 38 per cent of goods ordered through the net did not arrive at the specified time and 17 per cent did not arrive at all.

It is not surprising, therefore, that some people dismiss the internet out of hand. But complete cynicism is as out of place as the starry-eyed enthusiasm of late 1999. Even mobile phones met consumer resistance in the 1980s, when they were the size of a brick and were seen as rather laughable yuppie accessories.

It is time to put the internet in its proper context. Technology experts will have to excuse the next section. But explaining the basics helps us understand why the net seems so exciting and all-pervasive and why investors believed it would be the key to their fortunes.

The background of the net

The internet is essentially just a means for linking computers and enabling their users to share information. A computer in London might be linked with one in New York, which in turn is linked with one in Frankfurt, one in Tokyo and so on. Draw a series of lines between those cities and you can pretty soon see why the net is also often referred to as the World Wide Web.

The internet is modern proof of that old saying that 'two heads are better than one'. If you need to know the answer to a question, there is someone out there who can tell you. Before the internet, your best hope would probably be the *Encyclopaedia Britannica*. Now you can effectively gain access to 1,000 encyclopaedias in a minute. Indeed, *Encyclopaedia Britannica*'s traditional business was destroyed by the net – it is now no longer available in book form but can be read online.

Anyone who wants to put information on the web can publish it on a website. Each website will have its own address – all those https and wwws are the internet equivalent of house numbers, street numbers and postcodes.

Of course, just because the information is on a website doesn't mean it's easy to find, any more than we could find the right John Smith in the telephone directory. There are millions of websites already, even though the internet is less than a decade old.

The key step in general use of the internet was the development of the search engine. This is a piece of software that searches all known websites for selected key words or phrases. For example, when my wife came home from giving birth, she had a craving for pea soup. None of our cookbooks had a recipe. So I logged on to the internet, selected pea soup as a category and, sure enough, found several potential recipes.

Each user of the net can also have his or her own address, which enables them to exchange messages known as electronic mail, or e-mail, with any computer user on the planet.

All this information comes down the telephone line and can arrive in an instant. From the point of view of human communication, this is an enormous step forward. It is true that internet communications can, like telephone calls, be intercepted and access to certain websites can be blocked off. But any censor attempting to do this would face a Sisyphean task. There are not enough hours in the day to monitor everybody's e-mails and, as soon as you block off one website, it is the work of a moment to create a new site with a different address. When Sky News was covering the fall of Slobodan Milosevic, the presenters were regularly receiving reports by e-mail from ordinary Serbs in Belgrade. That would not have been possible ten years ago.

This ability to exchange ideas freely was the key inspiration behind those who developed the web. Indeed, some of the original web pioneers still resent its commercialisation. But the internet can be immensely useful for businesses. By allowing the instant transfer of information between all parts of a company and between a company and its suppliers and customers, the internet allows the economy to function better, rather as a car engine that has been properly tuned will run more smoothly.

Take a transport company with a fleet of delivery trucks. With the help of the internet, it can track its trucks wherever they go. When a new delivery is required, the computer can automatically select which truck is closest to the pick-up point and instruct the driver to go there. The result: fewer trucks will be on the road and fewer will be travelling empty. That will allow the business to save money on fuel and wages.

Or take a manufacturing company. In the old days, it would be required to hold a large amount of stocks to cover unexpected orders. But now the company can keep track of how many goods it has sold, when the next supplier's shipment is due and if there is the prospect of a shortfall, in which case it can instantly alert the supplier to step up delivery of new goods. The result: less capital tied up in stock levels. The freed capital can be used in more profitable projects.

Within companies, there can be scope for considerable cost savings. That term, alas, is a euphemism for job losses. A whole layer of administrative staff and middle managers – traditionally used to transmit information from top executives to the workforce and from one company to another – can be replaced. In theory, the remaining employees can be more productive. They can communicate with their office and work on their computers from home, on the train, on the plane. They can send and receive documents in an instant, without the need for overnight courier delivery or bulky faxes.

Of course, the internet also allows employees to spend all day sending their friends e-mails, surfing the net for porn, shopping with Amazon.com, playing computer games, listening to sports commentaries and all the rest. Some game sites even have the equivalent of a panic button – at the approach of a boss, one click of the mouse and something work-related (like a spreadsheet) appears on the screen. Employers are beginning to counter this problem by developing ways of monitoring how their employees use the web.

Making money from the web

The first step is to charge people for getting access to the net – after all, you need software, some hardware (a box called a modem) and a telephone line to do so. Internet service providers (ISPs) attempt to make a profit from this process. They either charge a flat monthly fee for access to the net, or take a percentage of the money earned by the telephone companies every time you dial in.

The good news is that internet access in the UK has been showing phenomenal growth. In September 2000, according to research group MMXI Europe, 11 million Britons were using the internet from home, an increase of 3 million from October 1999. The average time such users spent on the net increased from 4 hours 17 minutes a month to 5 hours 47 minutes over the same period.

The bad news about being an ISP is that it is a commodity-style business. It does not matter two hoots to the average user how they gain access to the net – all the services are pretty much the same. So most users are going to choose the service with the lowest cost. That puts endless downward pressure on the prices charged by ISPs and thus on their profits. A month after AOL launched its £15 a month unmetered service, for example, Freeserve came in with a £12.99 a month offer.

So ISPs have also attempted to become portals. A portal, as the name suggests, is a doorway to other services. This might simply be news (while users are reading the news online, they are running up their phone bill). It might be a chatroom or discussion group (if you make friends online, or you are hooked on the discussions, you will stay loyal to your ISP). Or the portal might give you the chance to buy particular goods and services, in which case the ISP will share some of the seller's revenue.

The sale of goods and services – e-commerce – is one of the most exciting potential uses for the internet. A purchaser can see details of goods from all over the world with the help of the net, and can choose the best product at the lowest price. No more traipsing through shopping malls or down the high street in search of goods only to find they are sold out. Just click on an image on screen and in a few days, the product will be at your door. Sellers can advertise their wares without the expense of owning a vast range of shops. So they can offer goods at lower prices than their high-street counterparts.

But of course, you can say all the above about the mail order business, which has been in existence for a long time and has only got a small proportion (around 10 per cent) of the retail market. Mail order has traditionally been seen as a low budget product for the lower income groups – not the type of people who tend to own a computer.

This gives internet retailers an image problem. You don't tend to hear people at Islington dinner parties boasting about how they got their clothes from the Kay's or Littlewoods catalogue. There may come a day when a computer will have all our vital statistics and can thus show us how clothes will look on a 3-D model of ourselves. Until then, most women (and quite a few men) will want to try clothes on before they buy them.

Books and CDs are a different matter – the product is standardised. Indeed, the net offers great advantages for those whose tastes are outside the mainstream. If your interest is eighteenth-century Serbian history or

Nigerian drum music, you are much more likely to find what you want on the net than at the average high street store.

In the UK, internet shopping is definitely growing fast. A survey by the research group Experian found that, between January and November 2000, the number of people buying goods and services over the net increased from 2.26 to 4.7 million, with 1.45 million consumers making four or more purchases. But even if someone orders books or clothes through the internet, the retailer still has to have somewhere to store the goods and still has to use a van to deliver them to your home. That diminishes the cost advantages.

US retailer Amazon.com (in the UK, the site is Amazon.co.uk) has been a great success in establishing its brand name in the book trade. And the service does appear to be good; books arrive quickly and there is an enormous choice. (It would be sad if it were too successful; there is something about a bookshop that a website cannot replicate: they are temples of modern civilisation which need to be preserved.) But at the time of writing Amazon has shown no signs of making a profit. It has resolutely refused to settle on one line of business, diversifying from books to CDs and then to more general merchandise. All it has proved so far is that you can sell lots of goods if you sell them cheaply enough. It has not proved you can create a viable business by doing so.

If your main selling point is your cheapness, your profit margins are likely to be thin. Companies have developed software that can search through all the retailers on the net and inform users of the lowest price available. Great news for consumers, but not so good for businesses.

Delivering non-physical goods is, potentially, a much more exciting use of the internet. Why wait for the morning's newspaper when you can read the news, as it happens, on your favourite paper's website?

The net can also replace activities that previously involved long and tedious battles with the phone systems of large corporations, involving the pressing of a series of numbers but the total absence of human communication. Ordering airline tickets, for example, is a task that can easily be achieved via the internet. The user can check flight times and prices and pick the one best suited to his or her budget. The same is true for other travel items, such as car rental or train journeys. The snag, however, is that travel agency is not a high margin business. When people buy plane tickets or trade shares over the web, they expect to be able to do so more cheaply than over the telephone or by post. Prices are forced down and any cost savings made by the companies concerned are simply passed through to the consumer. That is one of the beauties of capitalism; but it makes life much more difficult for investors.

This squeeze on prices is hard to break because it is so easy to set up an internet company. 'Virtually all the dotcoms had no barriers to entry,' says David Bowen, chief executive of Net Profit, a publishing and research company that specialises in electronic business. 'Even Amazon.com's model could be replicated very easily.'

The ideal would be to create an upmarket dotcom company, a trick that Lastminute.com is trying to pull off. It is not really aiming to be the cheapest ticket provider but to offer all sorts of goods and services to those who want to do something, or go somewhere, in a hurry.

Making money out of the delivery of information and entertainment over the net is also proving a difficult task. People are happy to read their newspaper over the internet; they are just not happy to pay for it (with the exception, in the US, of the *Wall Street Journal* whose readers clearly see a financial benefit in getting the latest stock market news as quickly as possible). The early marketing efforts of net companies can now be seen as a mistake. The idea was to offer something for free to get people used to the service. Once they had learned to love the service, then consumers would be willing to pay. But almost everybody followed the same strategy so that when one company tried to charge, consumers could simply switch to others that did not.

For a while, traditional newspapers were in a state of panic. How could they compete against services that were free and far more immediate than a paper product delivering yesterday's news? Many accordingly spent heavily on developing their own websites.

But in fact, while many websites have come and gone, newspapers and magazines are still going strong. 'As yet there has been no mindset change, information on the web must be free, whereas consumers do expect to pay for information printed on dead trees,' says Rob Golding of Tornado-Insider.

Even Stephen King, one of the most popular authors in the world, came unstuck when he tried to publish a book over the internet. He started to publish a novel, *The Plant*, in chapter form. Readers were asked to pay $1 a chapter (later $2) but King operated an 'honour system'; there was nothing to stop someone downloading the text for free. Alas, there turned out to be little honour among King's readers and he abandoned the project when too few paid up.

Music has been the key battleground between the interests of business and the 'free lunch' attitude of many net users. Programmes like Napster allow users to share their music files in a format called MP3, a sort of hi-tech version of taping your friends' records. It proved amazingly popular, attracting 65 million users in 18 months. But if you can get the stuff for free, why buy it from a store? *The Economist* reported that a record store near the campus of Syracuse University saw its monthly sales fall by 90 per cent. This raised a more fundamental issue than a newspaper publishing a free online version of itself. In most cases, the artists and recording companies who published the music had not given permission for it to be copied. Unsurprisingly, the recording companies, and bands such as Metallica, sued for breach of copyright.

At the time of writing, Napster had lost one US court case in the issue. But it looked as if it had changed the business model for the music industry. MusicNet was formed by Bertlesmann, EMI, and AOL Time Warner with the aim of selling music to web users and Yahoo, a US portal, had teamed up with Vivendi of France and Sony of Japan, with a similar aim. What the companies do not know yet is how much consumers will be willing to pay for music online. And the free model is not yet dead. Napster keeps a central register of users and the songs they have on their central register. Close down Napster and you destroy the heart of the system. But later technology such as Gnutella achieves the same feat without a central register – and so would be virtually impossible to shut down.

Online advertising

If consumers come to expect something for free, how do you make money out of them? One obvious answer is advertising. After all, adverts are how most existing media make most of their money. But there is a problem with internet advertising. When you read a paper or watch a TV programme, the adverts are included with the package; it's hard not to notice at least some of them. With the internet, some of the same effect can be achieved by placing banners on the website. But at the current state of technology, this does not allow for very sophisticated adverts – little more than the company's name. To get something more detailed, users must click on the banner with their mouse. However, they then have to wait for the advert to download, a process that uses up valuable time and computer memory. Few users have the patience to do so. According to *The Econo-*

mist, 'click-though' rates had fallen from 1 per cent in 1997 to 0.4 per cent in 2000.

A report by PriceWaterhouseCoopers found that online advertising revenues in the third quarter of 2000 were up just 10 per cent on the previous quarter – a sharp slowdown in the previously exponential growth rate. And a report from a group called Leading Web Advertisers in 2000 found that 80 per cent of the ad space on leading websites goes unsold. All this brings us back to square one. If consumers are unwilling to pay money for information and content received over the internet, and advertising is ineffective, how are businesses supposed to make a profit? The answer is rather depressing.

So far, the surest way of making money out of consumers from the internet is pornography. This has some great advantages as a net business. For consumers, they no longer face the embarrassment of reaching for the top shelf at the newsagent. Nor do they have to wait while the disapproving video store clerk searches for the tape of *Danish Nurses On the Job.* They can get hold of the goods they want from the privacy of their own room.

And because these goods are difficult to obtain elsewhere, they have a scarcity value that businesses can exploit. If you don't send your credit card details, you don't get to see the pictures. Plenty of people are willing to pay for the privilege.

From B2C to B2B

All of the above analysis refers to business-to-consumer transactions, what are known in the trade as B2Cs. By the time UK investors were getting excited about the likes of Lastminute.com, US investors had already shifted their focus to business-to-business or B2B models.

Think about a big manufacturer that has to buy components from all over the world. It has relationships with dozens, perhaps hundreds, of suppliers round the world. Can it be sure it is getting the best prices at any given moment, or that its suppliers will have a sufficient stock of rotary widgets when they are needed? By putting all those relationships on the internet, it can get instant information about prices and stocks. It can find out about alternative suppliers, who might offer better quality or charge lower prices. It can also be much better informed about the status of its orders and deliveries. 'If you send a package by Federal Express, you can now check where it is in their system by looking on their website,' says David Bowen of Net Profit. That saves money at both ends; the customer doesn't have to ring FedEx's call-centre to chase after the package and FedEx doesn't have to employ someone to take that call.

Supporters of B2B claim that big manufacturers will be able to use the net to save billions of pounds. In many industries, companies have grouped together in exchanges, linking those who buy or sell timber or steel. In the food retailing industry, Tesco has set up an online exchange with ten other retail groups, including Kingfisher, Marks & Spencer and French businesses. The groups control 30,000 stores between them with sales of almost £200bn a year.

Ian Smith, managing director of software company Oracle UK, explained the concept behind exchanges.[3] 'Here is an opportunity to do what we call a reverse auction – instead of going around asking each supplier to submit a bid against a particular specification, a process that can take months – they go on the internet, they describe the specification of product they want, the volume they want, the likely buying price – and they just set a time for anyone around the world to bid.'

Some exchanges have been established by the big companies in the industries concerned; others have been set up independently with the hope of grabbing a slice of B2B activity. One estimate by Nat Schindler, an analyst at the investment bank Credit Suisse First Boston, found that total business-to-business activity worldwide was $47,000bn or $47trn. Schindler thought that some 65 per cent, or $30trn, of this activity would eventually be conducted over the net. B2B exchanges could grab 40 per cent of that, or business worth $12trn. Even if they charge 3 per cent per transaction, that would add up to fees of $400bn a year. Already, the Gartner group estimated that $23bn of goods passed through electronic marketplaces in 1999. The B2B model may well help many businesses cut their costs. Whether or not it justifies enormous stock market valuations for B2B companies is another matter.

It seems likely that the exchanges controlled by the multinational corporations rather than the independents will control the bulk of the business. Why would the multinationals allow some of the hoped-for cost savings to be taken by outsiders?

Nor is the B2B model wholly benign. To the extent that large manufacturers get lower prices from B2B exchanges, it will be at the expense of their suppliers, many of which will also be quoted on the stock market.

This has caused some alarm in the small business sector. 'What you will be getting is world-class leading UK companies ignoring small businesses who produce goods at reasonable prices,' said Stephen Alembritis, head of policy at the Federation of Small Businesses.[4] The corporate sector as a whole may be no better off.

And, in any case, the cost savings may not be that large. Most suppliers will tell you that large companies are already less than generous on price. And it may not be in the long-term interest of big business to get the lowest possible costs if the result is a loss of quality.

One sceptic of the B2B revolution is Peter Wilson, who runs a small paper business. 'We are giving the internet every chance, and have a website (paperline.co.uk), but we don't expect to get any business from it, because our customers, people like doctors' practice managers, chefs, garage managers, and the like will never in a million years sit down and waste twenty minutes logging on to internets to order £80–100 worth of goods.

'All these guys who go on about B2B being the next great white hope are mistaken. So much of business is driven by personal relationships, not the ease of access to other suppliers, prices etc. Our customers are called upon every day of the week, both personally by sales people and by phone, so an internet relationship would have to have an amazing USP [unique selling proposition] to score. The trouble about the internet is that it destroys margins, thereby destroying service levels, because it can only sell on price. As such, it is difficult to see how such a business model can ever deliver profits, never mind the sort of profits journalists seem to think they can make next year or in years to come.'

However, analysts and big firms remain optimistic. The administrative costs of buying and selling goods will be reduced as will the need to hold stockpiles or inventories – since suppliers and customers will be instantly aware of the other's needs and capabilities. General Electric, the giant US corporation, said in 2000 it was hoping to cut around 15 per cent from its cost base in each of the following two years.[5]

Picks and shovels

By early 2000, some analysts were already starting to look askance at B2C and even B2B business models. Instead, they used an analogy from the nineteenth century. The people who made money out of the Klondike gold rush, they said, were not the prospectors who took enormous risks to pan for gold but the businesses that sold them the equipment to do so – the picks and shovels.

The companies that would make money from the internet, analysts reasoned, would be those that built the infrastructure that made the system work. So the focus shifted to the groups that supplied fibreoptic cables (down which internet data would travel), microchips, routers and all manner of other devices. These companies produced things that the average consumer or businessman would never see but which nevertheless ensured that information flowed through the net.

In the UK, the leading groups were ARM, which designs chips, Bookham Technology, whose chips generate and control light signals in fibreoptic networks, and Baltimore Technologies, whose encryption software ensures that internet transactions are secure. The share price of these companies soared in early 2000, catapulting the companies into the FTSE 100 index.

This, alas, proved to be a mini-version of the dotcom bubble. Investors extrapolated the growth rates of these companies into the never-never, forgetting that a) they might have competitors and b) demand for goods such as fibreoptic cables might lag behind supply. Even those businesses were much more sound than many of their dotcom predecessors, investors who bought in mid-2000 had a very unhappy experience. Bookham shares, which were floated at £10 and went to £54 were back at £3 by early April 2001.

In the end, picks and shovels may not have been the most appropriate analogy. Picks and shovels stayed the same. The problem with the technology industry is that it changes so quickly; a product can seem highly sophisticated when it is first introduced only to become a commodity widget five years later. One company's technological edge can disappear overnight if a new, smarter business arrives.

The mobile net

The link between mobile telephones and the internet is, for some investors, even more exciting than the computer market. Only a small proportion of the population has a personal computer, which, despite price falls, represents an expensive purchase for the average family. The majority of the population now has a mobile phone, thanks to two developments – the decision by most airtime providers to virtually give away the phones themselves and the development of pay-as-you-go call charges. Individual calls may be more expensive with a pay-as-you-go system but the purchaser has security – he or she knows their maximum liability. This is particularly important for parents who want to buy a mobile phone for their teenagers.

But we are only at the first phase of mobile phone usage. When the third generation of mobiles comes into use, the hope is that phones will become the main driver of net usage – the mobile net.

In commercial terms, the key attraction of the mobile net is that companies will know who you are and where you are (with the help of another technological development: a short-wave radio system called Bluetooth which allows one machine to communicate with another). You will be walking down the high street when you pass the local Italian restaurant – it will message you to let you know that Lasagne, your favourite dish, is on special today. The local cinema can message you with video clips of the current releases. You can check the traffic and weather for your area, look up the sports score for your favourite teams, monitor the news and trade shares. As you sit on the bus, you will be able to shop via your mobile phone – m-commerce as it is known in the jargon.

In the future, you will never be alone with a mobile phone. This may seem like a vision of heaven to some. It will definitely be the recipe for lots of junk e-mail. Not to mention traffic accidents. It's bad enough that both pedestrians and car drivers are already nattering away to their friends and partners. Just imagine the chaos that will ensue when they are tapping away on the keyboard trying to sell shares and book cinema tickets.

The industry also needs to overcome some basic design hurdles. Modern phones are deliberately light and small enough to fit in a pocket – consumers like them that way. But small phones mean small screens and small keyboards. That makes it awkward to send messages. It also makes watching any kind of entertainment on screen an unrewarding experience.

The arrival of Wap phones (wireless application protocol) turned out to be a disappointment. Wap is a system that reconfigures internet pages for the mobile phone screen. In theory, it makes it possible to surf the net from the garden or Clapham High Street. In practice, the combination of net and mobile phone unreliability made it a slow and unrewarding experience. By October 2000, Wap phones had attracted just 2 million subscribers, not the 10 million the industry had expected.

In theory, the third generation of mobile phones will change all this.

Certainly that is what persuaded the big mobile phone companies to pay billions for licences in the UK and Germany and to spend further billions developing the infrastructure to build the service. Third generation phones will have much greater capacity to receive data at faster speeds.

There is clearly a market for mobile-phone messaging systems. Many businesspeople already have pagers, while teenagers appear to relish a further chance to communicate. A short messaging system in Japan called I-mode has been enormously successful.

What the industry doesn't yet know is whether people really have an appetite to receive information and conduct transactions over a mobile phone. In November 2000, NTT DoCoMo, the Japanese mobile phone giant, warned that third generation technology would prove unsuitable for carrying large video or sound clips, one of the big hopes of the industry. The clips would use up too much of the radio spectrum and would prove too costly to transmit.

Telecom shares fell sharply in the summer and autumn of 2000 as investors started to have doubts about the industry's ability to make a profit from the third generation phones. The companies themselves started to scale back their ambitions – the Italian and Swiss auctions proved grave disappointments to the companies concerned as the bidders pulled out. Within a year, the mobile telecom industry went from being the great global growth industry to a sector plagued by doubts about its high debt levels and business strategy.

This is one element of the new era that has not yet proved it will provide 'easy money'.

Internet banking

Banking is another area where the internet is widely expected to play a big role. From the point of view of the banks, dealing with customers over the net is a lot cheaper than having to employ tellers and maintain branches. Because of those cost savings, banks can offer more attractive rates on deposits and charge less on borrowings.

From the customer's point of view, using an internet bank saves a lot of time travelling to the bank and standing in queues. They can also bank when they want to – whether it is first thing in the morning or last thing at night. 'We're all bank managers now,' as Robbie Coltrane proclaims in an advert for Barclays.

But you cannot get cash out of a personal computer or pay in a cheque. That requires a machine or a branch. Inertia is also a powerful force in the banking market – Britons are supposed to change their spouses more often than their banks. There is a lot of hassle involved in changing all those standing orders and direct debits, and most of us can't be bothered.

The type of people who will change to an internet banking account will be those who always chase the best offer. You can recruit them for a while but they'll be off as soon as someone offers them a better deal. The result has been a plethora of 'loss-leading' deals. In October 2000, for example, Egg said it would cut its introductory interest rate to zero for the next six months while another internet bank, Cahoot, agreed to pay 7.1 per cent on current accounts, more than a percentage point above the base rate. In neither case had the bank a hope of making money on such deals.

But that was not the point. Once the customers had joined up for the service, the hope was they would buy all sorts of other products, such as unit trusts, consumer loans and the like. However, such cross-selling, as it is called, is a strategy many banks have pursued with little success. Customers may cash their cheques at Barclays but they tend to buy their unit trusts from Fidelity or Jupiter and their insurance from General Accident or Royal & Sun Alliance.

At the time of writing, internet banks had yet to prove they can succeed in cross-selling where their long-established rivals have failed. Egg, one of the pioneers, was even thinking of setting up a branch network. Analysts were starting to take the view that the net would benefit existing banks, by lowering their costs, rather than their virtual rivals. Lazy customers would simply migrate to the net with their existing bank. That would give them flexibility, while allowing them to retain the ability to get cash out and pay money in. There is a direct parallel here with those business trying to make money from businesses selling information and entertainment on the net. It is easy to dream up services that seem attractive to consumers; much less easy to work out how to make a profit from them.

Founding internet companies

Back in mid 1999, both investors and entrepreneurs saw all of the above areas as golden business opportunities. They queued up to send business plans to banks and venture capitalists and to find their place in a golden future. After all, this was a new industry. So almost every business area could be discovered anew. There was a dotcom book shop, but what about dotcom CDs? Sport news? Property sales? Second-hand cars? There could have been few people who did not sit down for a minute and try to think of an idea that would make them an internet millionaire.

Some even got as far as producing a business plan, but many of them were muddle-headed. The ideas were grand but there was little attention to detail. According to Ajaz Ahmed, chairman of the technology consultancy AKQA: 'We always talk about a customer proposition. Companies need to think what makes something indispensable to a customer. Consumers are ruthless because they have so much choice. Too many people think there is a short cut to success, a "secret sauce". A lot of people dream of running their own business but everything is in the subtleties, the execution.'

Entrepreneurs also frequently had a totally unrealistic expectation of the potential size of their market. 'Whatever your universe is, say BMW owners, only a small number will have net access,' points out Ahmed. 'Of that number, only a small number will visit your site and of that number, only a small number will make a purchase.'

Another common trait was overconfidence. 'There was so much money around that people thought there could be no risk. I was at a seminar back in December 1999 and I said to the assembled entrepreneurs, "UK venture capitalists are becoming like American VCs, where they back ten companies in the hope that one will be successful. I suppose all of you think you will be the one, and not one of the nine." Their jaws dropped,' says Lucy Marcus of Marcus Venture Consulting. Her company provides expertise investing – it takes a stake in a business in return for providing advice, and venture advising – it helps investors who want to put money into the technology sector.

It is particularly difficult to spot the winners in a fast-changing industry like technology. Many more companies will fail than succeed. Research by Morgan Stanley Dean Witter found that just 5 per cent of the technology companies floated since 1980 have produced 77 per cent of the shareholder value.

So, given the poor hit rate, why were so many companies launched? It is easy to understand it from the founders' point of view (but see also Chapter 5). There was immense publicity about a new generation of internet millionaires. In the past, it used to take decades to build a successful business and have the chance to cash in. In the new economy, it could be done in less than two years – easy money indeed.

But the inevitable consequence of creating companies in haste was that the founders paid too little attention to building the business for the long term. 'If you look at the history of great businesses such as Microsoft or Intel, what they got right was the product,' says Ajaz Ahmed. 'That is the substance of the organisation, the packaging can come later. For some reason, people think packaging has become more important than substance.'

Ahmed says that some businesses became obsessed with fashion. 'Everyone is looking for trends or fads whether it is B2B or B2C. Everything is happening so fast that they aren't paying attention to detail. I've never known people be successful who pursue wealth for wealth's sake.'

The 'shoot for the moon' approach of trying to become the biggest business in the sector also caused a lot of problems. 'Why did anyone think that realistically you could grow a small company within twelve months to the size of companies that had been built over twenty years?' asks Lucy Marcus. 'You have to acclimatise, like a diver, or else you explode.'

George Colony, founder of Forrester Research, said that 'Many of the dotcom (leaders) seemed I would say hollow; they were unsophisticated, they had a lack of depth in business thinking, in comparison to the traditional CEOs. And so I began to think that many of the dotcoms in fact were what I call hollow dotcoms – that they were vapid, that they were not well run, that they were not well managed, that they were essentially being built to flip, being built to sell stock in and then move on to the next venture.'[6]

The flipping he refers to is a term adopted, inevitably, from the US. It refers to a practice whereby favoured investors can make a quick profit on their shares. Most commonly, key institutional clients of an investment bank were allocated shares in a hot new issue (from which the public were excluded, see Chapter 2). They then sold and took a quick profit when the shares started trading and soared to a seemingly inevitable premium.

But the more general point was made by one US venture capitalist. His view was simply this: 'The point is not to build a business. The point is to come to market.' His cynicism was understandable. For the founders of the company, building a business was not what would make them rich. The key was to persuade the stock market to give the business a high value, and then to sell off at least a portion of their holding.

For the venture capitalists who backed the dotcom companies, a quick profit was just as good (in fact, even better) than a slow one. The business of venture capital is investing in small, unquoted companies – it involves high risk, but usually high returns since the limited number of successes more than make up for the majority of failures. In a new industry, where the future was far from clear, it seemed to make sense to back as many companies as possible in the hope of finding the few winners.

But venture capitalists can only realise their profits if they have an exit route – either selling the business to a competitor or bringing it to the market. In the late 1990s, companies were floated far earlier in their life than they used to be, helped by stock exchanges that were eager to get the hottest new issues. 'Microsoft didn't float for ten years until it was a $150m revenue company,' points out Ahmed. 'But when you got the venture capital boys jumping on the bandwagon, all they cared about was flotation.'

The hard-headed venture capital industry both fuelled and fell victim to internet fever. Victor Basta is co-president of Broadview International, one of the largest venture capital groups, and a member of the firm's management committee. He started to notice that things were getting out of hand in the late 1990s. 'The valuation of companies being privately financed was creeping up to $150–$200m. Now in the US, 75 per cent of IPOs came to the market with a valuation of $250m or more but in Europe 75 per cent of IPOs had a valuation of $250m or less. A $500m flotation in Europe is a big number. But if you are valuing companies privately at $200m, you need to get it to $500m–$1bn on flotation for the venture capitalists to make money.' (Venture capitalists demand very high returns from the deals that succeed to compensate for the many failures.)

'What most people must have been betting on,' says Basta, 'is the total transformation of the equity markets within three to six months. European technology markets are today where Nasdaq was in the late 1970s or early 1980s. So they were betting markets would catapult seventeen years in three to six months.' That, he felt, was highly unlikely.

It also suggested that the industry was acting irrationally. 'If the fundamental value isn't there and you can't take the company public or sell it, then what you are doing as a venture capitalist is just writing a cheque,' Basta says. 'There was a philosophy in the industry that "This is hot, you have to be in it."'

Inevitably, like everybody else, venture capitalists struggled to keep up with a rapidly changing technological and economic outlook. 'When you get on to the detailed technology issues, you will have lost 90 per cent of non-specialist venture capitalists by that point,' says Basta. 'They will say "We back management", but good management is a necessary but not sufficient condition. If you have the wrong box, you're dead.' Basta says the venture capitalist's job gets harder and harder. 'You need the technical knowledge and global understanding, and the burden expands at an exponential rate.'

This irrationality was not confined to the UK. In the US, money flowed into the dotcom sector. According to Venture One, a US research group, around $65bn was ploughed into internet companies by venture capitalists between January 1998 and July 2000. At one point, seven separate pet websites were being funded. Given that the biggest cost of keeping a pet is pet food, which costs a lot to transport, this was not a good idea. Any potential savings to customers on price would be wiped out by postage charges.

The bubble bursts

Things really went wrong in March 2000. The Nasdaq Composite index in the US suddenly started to fall. Lastminute.com's flotation proved a disappointment to investors. When Boo.com failed in May, the mood among investors started to turn from unbridled enthusiasm to outright scepticism.

The odd thing from the UK's point of view was how brief the flurry of speculation appeared to be. The US had been indulging in internet fever for years, since the flotation of Netscape in 1995. It had already started to fall out of love with B2C companies and had moved on to B2B and fibre-optics groups. The UK telescoped all those changes in fashion into a few months.

'I was surprised at how quickly the market turned,' says Victor Basta. 'When it turned in the US, it immediately turned in Europe. Everybody talks about globalisation but globalisation is when everybody knows what's going on all the time. We've learned that markets dry up completely, they don't just drop.'

Suddenly, stock market investors and entrepreneurs started to focus on conventional measures like profits and cashflow. Investors focused on gross margin – does a business actually sell its goods and services at a significantly higher price than it costs to create them? 'Gross margin really does matter because it tells you the kind of business you're in,' says Basta. If the company had good gross margins, there was hope that, once its start-up costs had been paid, it might make some money.

Entrepreneurs who had previously thought that money was no object had suddenly to worry about paying their bills. It was a nasty shock for some. 'There was an era when no one said no to these people,' recalls Lucy Marcus. 'My mother once said, "It's one thing to build sandcastles in the air, it's another to move in."' Some felt let down by the venture capitalists who had previously been so generous. 'I used to explain that people don't just give you money because you have a nice idea, they want to make money,' says Marcus.

Feast turned to famine. The big advertising campaigns that marked the early stages of the dotcom era were scaled back. According to media research company AC Nielsen MMS, spending by dotcom companies on traditional advertising fell from £35m in March 2000 to £26m in October.

The key measure was now 'burn rate' – how quickly were the companies burning through the cash piles they originally raised from the venture capitalists or the market? The slower the burn rate the better, from everyone's point of view. A rapid burn rate meant that the company was making heavy losses. It also meant that the company would soon require new funding. But if the company were making heavy losses, then investors would not want to throw good money after bad. Like blue touchpaper, when the burning stopped, there would be an explosion.

Many dotcom companies found themselves on a kind of death row waiting to be put out of their misery. There was now little hope of flotation for all but the best prospects. In a way, it was rather unfair; the businesses had been started with the original expectation of losing money for a while, and now suddenly they were expected to change plans. That, alas, is the danger of depending on the kindness of venture capitalists.

'Our early plans were to lose money for the first three years,' says Robert Norton of the health and beauty products group Clickmango. With the help of *Absolutely Fabulous* star Joanna Lumley, Clickmango hoped to be the pre-eminent dotcom group in the beauty treatment area, a sort of Body Shop of the net. 'We performed better than the plans had forecast, we were ahead in sales terms and ahead on customer acquisition. Our initial money should have run out in June but in fact we stretched it to September.'

Clickmango was much mocked for its boardroom, an inflatable circular pink structure held up by wires and, rather too symbolically for comfort, hot air. 'The costs of that meeting room was equal to one built from breezeblocks,' says Norton. 'In a dotcom culture, people wanted to try something new, staff were working long hours and there needs to be greater concern about the office environment. When you're building a team, you have only yourself and the working environment to sell to staff.'

Norton says his company was not extravagant. 'We were not a business of excess. We had just thirty people on the staff and our burn rate was under £100,000 a month by the end. Our office space was incredibly cheap, we were in a warehouse building in the East End. In the US, three-quarters of the seed money is spent on marketing at the average dotcom, but we spent only 10 per cent.'

However, Clickmango still needed more money if it was ever to get to the stage of making a profit. 'We always said we would need £10m to take us to breakeven over 2–2½ years,' he recalls. But while venture capitalists were falling over themselves to fund him just a year previously, they were unwilling to do so in the summer of 2000. 'The problem was the bottom dropped out of comparable companies, like Mother Nature, in the US,' says Norton. Not only could Clickmango not raise £10m, even a rescue plan involving funding of just £300,000 proved impossible.

It was an incredibly wild and short ride. The Clickmango site was only launched in April, the decision to wind it down came in June and it was shut down in September. Norton and Rowland opted for an orderly withdrawal. 'We closed the business down so it did not go bankrupt and honoured all our orders,' says Norton. In retrospect, the company should have taken advantage of the enthusiasm for dotcoms while it lasted. 'We could have raised more money in December/January but we didn't foresee how quickly the climate would change.'

Some dotcom businesses started to look around for a strategic investor or for a bigger business that might buy them for their brand name or their technology. Jungle.com, which sells computers and games, was bought by Great Universal Stores for £337m in September 2000; earlier in the year, there were plans to float it on the market with a value of £700m.

Jungle.com was a rarity because, in truth, pure e-businesses had little to offer. All they had was a not very successful brand name. 'E-commerce was not much to do with technology,' says Victor Basta. 'There's really no solution for a lot of these companies. They would like to get sold or get a strategic investor. But they think that because their shares have fallen 80–90 per cent, they will be seen as a bargain. But they still trade at a huge multiple of revenues. And it is not possible in a 9 per cent margin business to justify that valuation.'

The summer and autumn of 2000 saw a steady steam of net companies give up the ghost. In the US, *Fortune* magazine reported that 124 dotcom companies bit the dust between January and early December 2000. In the UK, prominent casualties included Boxman, a compact disc retailer, Easier, a property service and thestreet.co.uk, a financial news website. Ready2Shop, a women's fashion shop created by two journalists (for a while, their pictures were all over the tube), went 'into hibernation'.

Easier, an online property group, was an interesting case. Its business plan was to allow users to buy and sell houses for free and then to sell information about those people to financial services groups. The companies that bought the information found that it did not lead to as many product sales as they had hoped.[7] The shares floated on the market at 150p, jumped to 330p, before falling to 20.5p when the company abandoned its plans. The business did not run out of money but the founders decided not to throw good money after bad. Instead, the group decided to become a cash shell[8] and look for a new business to buy.

Perhaps the ultimate example of a dotcom collapse was Wetnose.com, a pets e-tailer that went bust without selling a single item, but not before spending £1.5m on a website and printing 250,000 catalogues. As Sherlock Holmes might have said: 'It was the strange case of the dog that did not trade.'

This collapse in confidence may only be the end of the first phase of the internet. There is still plenty of belief in the long-term potential of technology companies. 'I still believe that the tech sector will be the best place to invest long term as the twenty-first-century economy is built and I am especially excited by the opportunities arising from the convergence of web, broadband and wireless technologies,' said private investor Steve Bennetts.

Venture capitalists are still willing to fund technology companies – they're just being more selective. 'Even now with things falling back, you still have a hundred times more chance being funded as a technology company than as anything else,' says Lucy Marcus.

And although those people who invested at the top of the market might not think so, dotcom mania had its positive side. David Bowen of Net Profit says that 'It was always very clear that most of what was going on was nonsense and that the vast majority of dotcom companies had no prospects. It was also clear that investors had gone mad and were chasing each other. But dotcoms were very useful sacrificial lambs for the rest of the economy. All the interesting ideas, like e-commerce and auctions, were pioneered by dotcoms and have been adopted by the rest of business. It was a very useful process even though the people who were involved at the time weren't going to benefit in the long run.'

Internet companies and the overall economy

A bit like motherhood and apple pie, the internet is generally assumed to be a 'good thing'. It represents an improvement in the way mankind organises itself and should increase economic output and overall wealth.

But by how much? It is easy to forget that there have been a lot of technological advances over the last hundred years. The US National Academy of Engineering asked its members to rank the greatest technological innovations of the twentieth century – and the internet came thirteenth. The car, the aeroplane and refrigeration were all ranked higher.

The investment bank Goldman Sachs looked back at the era of electrification in the US,[9] a period of dramatic change in individual lives. Electricity brought light, warmth, entertainment, household gadgets and so on. The key period of electrification caused the US economy to have a higher economic growth rate than before. But it did not result in a rise in the proportion of the economy claimed by corporate profits – in fact, the profit share fell slightly.

And the share prices of electric utilities – the power companies that supplied the raw material for the new era – actually peaked, in relative terms, in 1900, well before the benefits of electrification were in full swing. The reason? Competition. As the industry became more efficient, it became possible for consumers to get power from outside their area. That abolished the local power monopolies, forced prices down and reduced profit margins – just as economic theory suggested would happen.

How does the internet compare with the electric era? It does seem that the growth in internet usage in the late 1990s coincided with a period in which US productivity showed a sharp improvement. Over the period 1972–95, labour productivity improved by 0.7 per cent a year. Between 1995 and 1999, it grew by 2.2 per cent a year. It was natural, in some people's eyes, to link the two.

Certainly it seems likely that technology had something to do with it. Figures from the US Department of Commerce show that the proportion of capital expenditure devoted to technology rose from 15 per cent in 1960 to 27 per cent in 1980 and 47 per cent in 1999.

But there is some dispute about how big a role technology played.

Robert Gordon of Northwestern University in the US has argued that the influence of the new economy may be an illusion.[10] First, he says that the acceleration of productivity in the late 1990s was largely due to cyclical effects. When an economy is expanding rapidly, firms tend to produce a lot more with the same (or slightly increased) numbers of workers. In short, output rises faster than employment, which makes the productivity numbers look good. When the economy is growing slowly or shrinking, in contrast, output falls faster than the labour force and the productivity numbers look bad.

Secondly, Gordon argues that one sector in particular, computer hardware, is responsible for the bulk of the productivity improvement. Manufacturers have undoubtedly been very successful at producing more powerful computers at lower cost. What has yet to be proved, argues Gordon, is that those computers have been used to improve productivity in the rest of the economy.

In contrast, two US Federal Reserve economists, Stephen Oliner and Daniel Sichel, say that technology spending has prompted the productivity improvement.[11] They argue that it was not until the mid 1990s that the actual stock of information technology equipment in the US was large enough to have an impact on overall economic growth.

A slight variant on this explanation comes from Jeremy Greenwood, professor of economics at the University of Rochester.[12] He argues that new technologies take time to be recognised as useful to be adapted to practical ends by the first wave of users and then to be adopted throughout the economy. It can take twenty years for this effect to come through – and in the early years productivity may fall as workers are re-trained in the new skills. Given that Greenwood puts the dawn of the IT age in 1974, that may explain the recent surge in productivity.

Note, however, that if these arguments are correct, the internet had very little to do with the productivity improvements. The internet only became widely used in the mid 1990s – so, on the Greenwood thesis, it will be 2015 before it shows up in the productivity statistics.

Even if the US has achieved a productivity miracle, thanks to the net, that does not prove the same effect has happened elsewhere. The UK's productivity record actually deteriorated in the late 1990s, with growth dropping to 1.3 per cent a year from 3.3 per cent in the first half of the decade.

Of course, there is plenty of hope that the UK and Europe will repeat the US achievement in future. Certainly, Europe has spent plenty of money on new technology. Morgan Stanley Dean Witter calculates that in Europe tech spending increased from 19 per cent of capital expenditure in 1992 to 28 per cent in 1999.[13]

A report from Richard Reid and Darren Williams of the investment bank Donaldson Lufkin & Jenrette argued that Europe would become the new economy story of the next decade 'with all that implies for higher productivity growth, an extended economic cycle and higher equity prices'. European companies were found to be only 12–18 months behind their US counterparts in terms of technology use.[14]

This debate is not helped by the difficulty of both defining and measuring productivity in some sectors of the economy. Productivity is a 'residual', a figure left over after other calculations have been made. First we calculate the volume of goods produced, then we figure out the number of people used to produce them. Any increase in the former that exceeds the increase in the latter is an improvement in productivity.

But this is not an easy calculation. First, we must measure what has been produced. In many cases, this figure is available in monetary terms, rather than in value terms. So statisticians must work out what part of the rise is due merely to inflation, and what part is an actual increase in output.

This in turn leads to a debate about quality improvements. I am writing this book on a Dell computer; the last time I wrote a book, it was on an original Amstrad. Although the Dell cost an awful lot more, it is far faster, has much greater memory and many more functions than the Amstrad. If you allow for quality improvements, the price of computing power has fallen.

But how exactly do you make that calculation? If the statisticians take an upbeat view of quality improvements, then inflation will look lower and growth and productivity will look higher. A more downbeat view makes a country's growth and productivity performance look worse.

Just to add to the confusion, how do you treat the service sector, which now comprises the vast bulk of the economy? It is far more difficult to count the output of a bank clerk than it is of a car worker. Does more necessarily mean better? If your hairdresser reduces the time for a trim from twenty to fifteen minutes, he or she will be able to deal with more clients each day. But greater speed might reduce the quality of the cut and other measures of customer satisfaction; some people like the feeling of being pampered. The hairdresser might end up losing clients as a result, or might get lower tips.

Similarly, as a journalist, would I necessarily become more productive by writing, say, 1,200 words a day instead of 1,000? What if the 1,200 words contain more mistakes? Or contain padding designed merely to enhance the length? And if everyone on the paper followed my example, would the readers necessarily want a *Financial Times* that was 20 per cent larger? Most people already struggle to read all the articles in their daily paper. All this means that we need to treat the relationship between the internet and productivity with caution.

A depressing forecast

Could the internet be so powerful that it now governs the economic cycle? That's the argument of a book[15] from the economics editor of *Business Week*, Michael Mandel.

Mandel argues that US economic growth in the 1990s has been driven by economic innovation, which in turn has resulted from the willingness of venture capitalists to finance start-up companies. The strength of the stock market has also played its part, in giving venture capitalists a profitable exit route and, thanks to share option plans, in encouraging key workers to quit their jobs with established companies to join new ventures.

All this has created a kind of virtuous circle in which more innovation drives the economy, which pushes up the stock market, which encourages more innovation. But a falling stock market would reduce the incentive for venture capitalists to finance start-ups and for workers to join them. That would slow the pace of innovation and, with it, productivity and economic growth.

At the same time, employees in the technology sector would lose their jobs and investors, alarmed by the stock market's fall, would cut their spending. The result would be depression. Worse still, central banks might not cut interest rates to solve the problem. That would be because established companies, relieved at the lack of competition from start-ups, would raise their prices. The result would be inflation. Central banks might even raise rates, making matters worse.

So the internet might yet kill the economic boom it helped create. Perhaps it's time for the government to launch a campaign: Is Your E-Mail Really Necessary?

4

Putting a Price on Shares

There was an element of the Klondike.

Stockbroker

A cynic, according to Oscar Wilde, is someone who knows the price of everything but the value of nothing; a true believer is someone who thinks he knows the value of an internet share.

The sudden public enthusiasm for shares in late 1999 and early 2000 was a distinctly selective process. Three sectors stood out – technology, media and telecoms, or TMTs for short (there's nothing the stock market likes more than an acronym). Technology's appeal was obvious, for all the reasons so far discussed. The telecoms sector had two big plus points – the rapid growth in mobile phone usage and the fact that the internet depended on data being sent down telephone lines. The enthusiasm for media stocks was less expected – indeed, for a while investors thought that the internet would be extremely damaging to media groups. Their products – newspapers, music, TV programmes – were being made available free via the net.

One deal turned that perception on its head. In January 2000, America Online, a US internet service provider, agreed to merge with Time Warner, the media giant that owned brands such as *Time* magazine, CNN and Warner Music. This seemed to mark a new phase in the internet's development – the marriage of distribution (AOL's direct line into American homes via their personal computers) and content (Time Warner's news and entertainment products). AOL needed products that would keep their customers loyal to their service; Time Warner's media brands fitted the bill. Time Warner needed to ensure that its brands were prominent in cyberspace.

Cynics would point out another reason for the deal: AOL was able to use its vastly overvalued shares to purchase a 'real' business with real revenues. In the long run, other, cheaper service providers might undermine its business model. But cynicism was not popular in the first quarter of 2000. Suddenly the content of every media group looked valuable, and the shares of such companies surged. The M joined the two Ts in stock market popularity.

An alternative classification was to describe the TMT stocks as 'new economy' stocks, capable of taking advantage of the information age. Everything else – from manufacturing companies through property groups to traditional retailers – was termed an 'old economy' business. They would see their businesses undermined by internet competition.

In early 2000, investors flocked to buy technology shares and technology funds. New themed unit trusts were launched to take advantage of retail investor enthusiasm for the sector. In March alone, £878m was invested in technology funds, 17 per cent of all the unit trust money invested in the month. The result was a sharply divided stock market. In March 2000, FTSE made the most sweeping changes ever to its blue chip 100 index. Out went nine 'old economy' companies, including some long-established industrial groups. Two of the country's biggest brewers, Scottish & Newcastle and Whitbread were relegated, along with the drinks group Allied Domecq. Out too went Imperial Tobacco.

In the new economy, it seemed that Britons were no longer so interested in drinking and smoking, but nor were they eating as much bread (Associated British Foods was another casualty), using electricity (Powergen was out) or taking a bath in London (Thames Water). Into the index came nine, largely new economy, groups, including Freeserve (Britain's first free internet service provider), Baltimore Technologies (the encryption software company) and Psion (the handheld computer group). It was as if the torch had passed from the old generation of companies to the new.

What was significant, however, was that many of the new economy companies had yet to build a sizeable business. In terms of employees, sales and profits, they were much smaller than the companies they replaced. The companies that fell out of the index made pre-tax profits of more than

£3.5bn; the companies that joined the index earned just £516m. Companies joined the Footsie when, by any normal criteria, there were still small businesses. In June 2000, fibreoptics group Bookham joined the index – its market capitalisation was around £6.5bn at its peak but its 1999 turnover was just £3.5m and it lost £16.7m that year.

FTSE had no choice about making the change. The FTSE 100 index is a measure of the stock market – not of business size. It is designed to include the 100 biggest companies by market value, rather than by profits or sales. Every quarter, FTSE works out the league table. Any company that is ranked 90th or higher automatically comes into the index; any company that is ranked 111th or lower automatically drops out.

Dropping out of the Footsie is not merely a matter of prestige. Those funds that track the FTSE 100 are forced to sell the stock. This can have a kind of 'double whammy' effect. When a company drops out of the index, it is usually because its share price has already been falling – demotion then gives the shares a further kick in the teeth. In a way, you can see this as the stock market doing its job. It is supposed to channel the savings of the nation into new projects – and what could be more up-to-date and exciting than the internet or mobile phones? Established companies like brewers and tobacco groups tend to be more involved in returning cash to shareholders than tapping them for new funds.

The March 2000 changes marked the triumph of 'growth' companies. Stock market investors have traditionally been divided into the 'value' and 'growth' schools. Although this is an over-simplistic split,[1] the former look largely for shares that seem cheap by traditional valuation methods, the latter concern themselves more with the prospects for profit growth, reasoning that the price will look after itself.

Value investors tended to have the better records during the 1970s and 1980s. This seemed to be because of the boom and bust economic cycles experienced during that period. During the bust phase, investors became too pessimistic about the prospects for so-called cyclical companies, in industries such as engineering and construction. Value investors accordingly bought such shares at that point, betting (correctly) that profits would recover when the cycle turned. At the height of the boom phase, investors got too optimistic about such cyclical companies. Value investors accordingly switched to 'defensives', shares in businesses which tend to prosper whatever the state of the economy. Examples would be food retailers or pub operators – people will always need to eat and drink.

But in the 1990s, the growth school gained the ascendancy. This was in part due to genuine technological change, which created a batch of new industries in areas such as media (BSkyB), software (Sage), or mobile phones (Vodafone). Such companies could regularly produce earnings per share growth of 20 per cent a year. Because of low inflation, such companies stood out; traditional business could only hope to grow their businesses in line with the overall economy, at around 5–6 per cent a year.

Investors started to demand growth at all costs. They were willing to pay very high ratings for companies that looked like delivering it. Take the standard valuation measure, the price–earnings ratio (p/e). This compares a company's profits with its share price. Analysts calculate the profits that are actually available to shareholders, after other charges such as tax and interest are taken off. This figure is known as the earnings. The earnings are then divided by the number of shares in issue to get the earnings per share. The final step is to divide the share price by the earnings per share to get the price–earnings ratio. For example, say that Megacorp has earnings of £30m and 300 million shares in issue; that will give it earnings per share of 10p. If its share price is 100p, its price–earnings ratio will be 10.

Normally speaking, the lower the p/e the better, as far as an investor is concerned. You can think of it as the number of years' profits an investor has to pay for the shares. If you bought Megacorp shares, and the company paid out its earnings in full to you each year, it would take you ten years to get your money back. For much of its history, the overall market has tended to trade on a p/e of between 10 and 20. Companies in fast-growing industries have traded on a rating above the top of that range; companies in sluggish industries have traded below it.

In the market of late 1999 and early 2000, the rules changed. A p/e of 20? Investors laughed at anything so paltry.

A table of the ratings for the various sectors appears every day on the back page of the *Financial Times*. It is compiled on the basis of rules decided by actuarial experts. For much of 2000, the column showing the p/e for the TMT sectors carried a little dagger symbol. This was because the actuaries in their wisdom had decided that a p/e of more than 80 must be the result of a statistical quirk – such as a big loss for the largest company in the sector. They were simply not prepared for the sight of investors willing to pay more than eighty years' earnings for a host of well-established stocks.

Many stocks at that time actually traded on ratings of three digits. In other words, if current profits were maintained, it would take more than a century for investors to get their money back. Long-term investing, indeed.

Now, of course, it may be quite sensible for some start-up companies to be valued on very high price–earnings ratios. When a company first edges from loss into profits, the latter figure might be quite small. But the market might correctly anticipate that profits will grow exponentially from that point.

The earnings growth rate of many technology companies was certainly very impressive in the late 1990s; the average growth rate was well above 20 per cent a year. The industry had many things going for it. Consumers were buying more personal computers, software and peripherals to take advantage of the internet; business was doing the same. The millennium bug scare prompted a wave of spending on computer consultancy.

An analysis by Bill Martin[2] of fund management group Phillips & Drew (admittedly a house of technology sceptics) argued that this surge in tech spending was primarily due to two factors: the surge in the overall level of economic growth and a fall in the relative price of technology goods. These factors are, he believes, unlikely to persist to the same degree. If US economic growth slowed to 3.1 per cent a year (from 4.4 per cent in the 1996–2000 period) and if the relative price of technology goods fell by 8.6 per cent a year (the average for the 1990s),[3] then IT spending growth for the 2001–5 period would, in cash terms, be 9.1 per cent a year. That's not at all bad, but compares with 17.7 per cent a year during 1996–2000. The profits growth of IT companies in these circumstances, Martin argues, would be just 6 per cent a year.

Investors bought technology stocks in late 1999 and early 2000 on the assumption that spending on IT goods would rise significantly, whatever the state of the economy. But did that actually make sense? A lot of the sales of 'new economy' companies were to old economy businesses. If the latter ran short of money, they would have to cut back on their capital expenditure; technology would suffer along with everything else. A report from investment bank Morgan Stanley Dean Witter[4] warned that tech spending had not been immune to the vagaries of the economic cycle in the past. In the recessions of the early 1980s and 1990s, tech spending growth fell to zero.

Technology's very success has made it more vulnerable than it was in the earlier recessions. 'In the old days, when tech was 5–20 per cent of your cap-ex budget and you had to cut back, you could leave it alone. Today, tech is approaching 50 per cent of cap-ex and that makes it more vulnerable to a cyclical slowdown, not less,' said Nancy Lazar of International Strategy & Investment Group.[5]

One can see these factors at play in two sectors that played a prominent part in dragging down technology stocks in late 2000 – personal computer manufacturers and chip markets.

Two of the fastest growing companies in the late 1990s had been Dell and Gateway, personal computer manufacturers that had prospered from the demand from consumers to surf the net. US personal computer sales grew by 20 per cent during 1997 and 18 per cent in 1998. But demand started to slow in 2000. By the third quarter of the year, Gartner Dataquest, a market research group, estimated that the annual growth rate had slowed to 12 per cent. In November 2000, Gateway warned that its Thanksgiving PC sales were 30 per cent below those of 1999. Why the slowdown? The most plausible reason was that most people who wanted to use a PC had already bought one. And those who had already bought PCs had little incentive to upgrade – their computers already performed all the functions they needed. After all, a computer is just another electronic box for the home, like a television, a video recorder or a stereo before it. And all those industries have followed the same pattern – rapid growth followed by intense competition and falling prices.

The same qualities apply in spades to the chip industry. Silicon chips are the key components of computers and mobile phones and demand has increased exponentially over the last twenty years. To meet this demand, many countries have set up chip manufacturing plants – it was a particular favourite of south-east Asian nations. The result? Although growth has been rapid, investors are forever looking forward to the moment when supply outstrips demand. The minute the industry starts to slow, shares in chip manufacturers get clobbered. They now see chip-making as a commodity business.

The problem with giving a company a very high growth rating is that eventually all industries pass out of their growth phase – once even smoke-stack industries like steel and chemicals were fast growers. And no company can grow at a rapid rate for ever. Eventually, sheer size starts to slow the business down; it is much harder to grow a £1bn company rapidly than it is to expand a £1m group. And it is even more difficult in highly competitive industries such as personal computer manufacturing or chip-making.

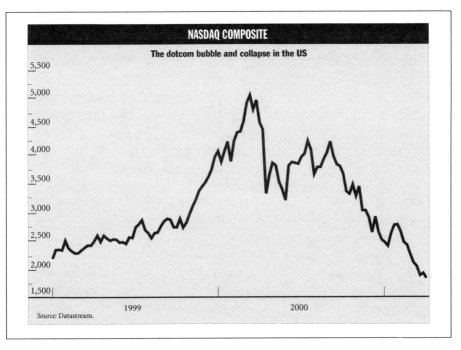

NASDAQ COMPOSITE

The dotcom bubble and collapse in the US

Source: Datastream.

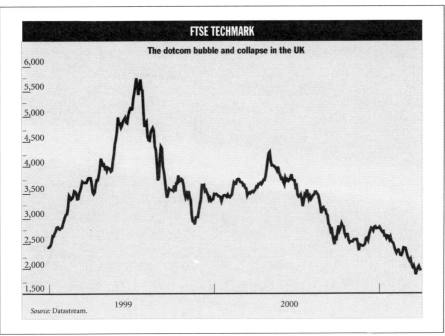

FTSE TECHMARK

The dotcom bubble and collapse in the UK

Source: Datastream.

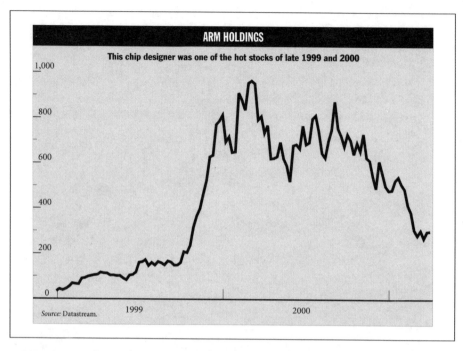

ARM HOLDINGS

This chip designer was one of the hot stocks of late 1999 and 2000

Source: Datastream.

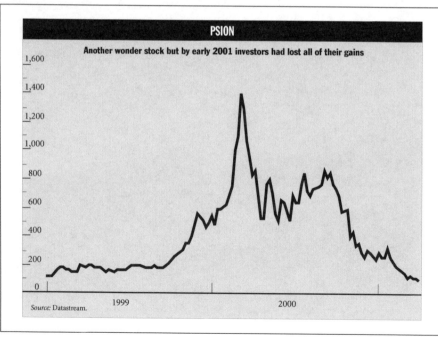

PSION

Another wonder stock but by early 2001 investors had lost all of their gains

Source: Datastream.

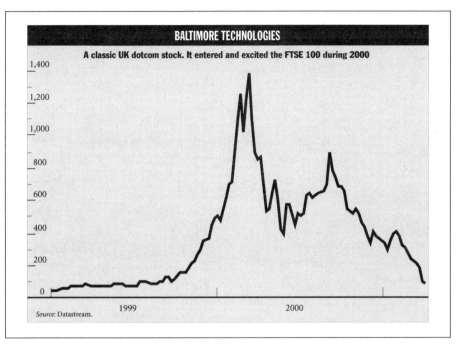

BALTIMORE TECHNOLOGIES

A classic UK dotcom stock. It entered and excited the FTSE 100 during 2000

Source: Datastream.

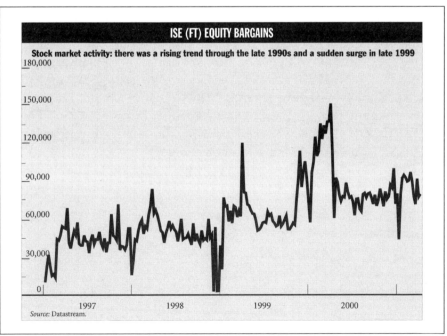

ISE (FT) EQUITY BARGAINS

Stock market activity: there was a rising trend through the late 1990s and a sudden surge in late 1999

Source: Datastream.

Surveys have shown that there is only a one in seven chance that a recognised high-growth tech stock can sustain that status for five years. And the chances that it can do so for ten years are just one in fourteen. Eventually, therefore, the company will start growing at the market average rate. And eventually the shares will trade on a market average rating. A fall in the rating will mean a fall in the share price. So these shares are, in a sense, accidents waiting to happen.

Take Sema, the Anglo-French software group. In February 2000, its shares traded at just over £18. The company was expected to produce earnings of 18.1p per share for the fiscal year 2000, so the shares were trading on a prospective p/e of around 100.[6] In November 2000, the company announced a profits warning. Second half profits for 2000 would be no higher than those for 1999. In other words, this was no longer a growth stock. The shares had drifted lower throughout the year as enthusiasm for TMT stocks had waned. On the day of the announcement, they fell a further 44 per cent to hit 346p. Investors who bought at the peak had lost 80 per cent of their money.

But note how that loss had occurred. After the warning, the most optimistic forecasts for the year were looking at 15p per share of earnings. That was only a sixth lower than previous estimates. The real killer had not been the decline in earnings but the decline in the p/e ratio from around 100 to 23; a fall of 75 per cent. When you buy a growth stock, you are implicitly betting that earnings will grow sufficiently fast to more than compensate you for the eventual de-rating of the shares. If the shares start on a p/e of 30 or so, you have a fighting chance. If they start on a p/e of 100, only the most exceptional companies will bale you out.

In December 2000, Sema's share price fall caused it to be relegated from the FTSE 100, along with fellow technology stocks Baltimore and Bookham. Breadmaker Associated British Foods returned to the index; man cannot live by technology alone.

Internet stocks

The price–earnings ratio is, of course, useless when it comes to valuing most internet companies. Most make a loss. Nor are revenues much of a guide since they are pretty scarce. To be fair, this would be true of most new businesses. But that would only be a problem for the founders and their bank manager. Internet companies created so many valuation problems because they floated on the stock market so early in their development.

One theoretical justification for the high valuations of some internet companies was the network principle. This states that the value of a network increases exponentially with the number of people connected to it. Say that you have a phone and your uncle has a phone. Useful for family crises, birthdays and Christmas but not that useful: how many times a year do you have to speak to your uncle? But if then your parents get a phone and your siblings get phones, you are likely to use your telephone much more often. The revenue of the phone company will grow sharply.

The same principle applies to an internet auction site. From the point of view of the sellers, they want their goods to be viewed by as many potential buyers as possible. From the point of view of the buyers, they want to see as many potential examples of the goods they want so they can select the best and the cheapest. Any business with a lead in this market should therefore quickly increase it. Say company A has 2 million users and company B 1 million users. Sellers on company A's site will have more potential buyers and therefore should see higher prices than company B's sellers – as they notice this, they will switch. That will reduce the potential range of goods for company B's buyers to look at; they will start to switch also. And so on.

The same theory, with a twist, can be applied to other internet businesses. In the real world, where physical geography is important, there can be room for lots of competitors. People in Blackburn will visit the pet foods store down the road rather than travel to, say, Leicester. But in the internet world, everyone can access the same store. What will make them visit the store? Name recognition. Once you have the brand name, you will also have the buying power to demand lower prices from your suppliers. That will make it easier to see off your competitors.

So there should be immense 'first mover' advantage to the company that gets its brand name out into the market. This takes us back to the reasoning that inspired Boo.com to spend so much money in such a short time. But, of course, there are a limited number of internet markets and there can be only one 'first mover' in each of them.

There were other arguments why some technology companies might have great economic advantages, and thus be worthy of a whole new valuation approach. One of the oldest laws of economics is that of diminishing returns. Imagine you are a farmer with only one tractor. Your logical move would be to cultivate the most fertile land first. Then, with your profits from that land, you can develop more land and so on. By the end, you will have reached the stoniest field – provided you can still earn enough from the crop to more than cover your costs, it is worth cultivating. But in terms of return on capital, this field will offer the lowest percentage return of all.

But this law may not apply to technology companies. If you are a company producing a software program, then it may well cost you a fair amount to create it, iron out the bugs and so on. But once you have created your product, the cost of making further copies is virtually zero. Your profit on the 1,000th copy should the same as your profit on the 100th.

The point may be valid, but it brings us back to the fundamental problem that is at the heart of this book. In essence, that argument says that companies can earn super-normal returns. But just as nature abhors a vacuum, free markets abhor super-natural returns. If it is possible to produce software at zero cost, then lots of people will produce it. The competition will drive prices down towards the marginal cost of production, i.e. zero.

There could be exceptions where there is a quasi-monopoly. In the case of Microsoft, its Windows operating system became accepted as standard. Software programs were written to interact with it. Once Windows was the operating system for nearly all computers, there was very little incentive for users to adopt any other standard – they would be restricted in their use of software and their computers would find it difficult to converse with other computers.

There will, however, be very few monopolies. And those that do exist will find themselves challenged by regulators, as Microsoft did in 1999 and 2000 when the US Justice Department brought a court case against its alleged anti-competitive activities.

One further argument is that the internet will help create a 'perfect market'. The idea of a perfect market is one of the simplifications that economists use to try to get a handle on the real world. In a perfect market, all consumers have perfect information and so are able to buy goods at the lowest price available. In the real world, of course, that rarely happens; very few people are willing to traipse for miles round various supermarkets in order to save a few pence on baked beans. In a perfect market, cars in the UK would not cost considerably more than cars on the continent – but they do.

But on the internet, in theory, consumers will be able to use a search engine that will find them the lowest available price for any good they care to buy. They will be able to do so without leaving their front room. A perfect market will therefore be created. That will force down prices, and profit margins, for the corporate sector.

Certainly there are some markets in which prices and margins have already been forced down sharply. In the book market, for example, Amazon.com has followed a strategy of undercutting its 'bricks and mortar' competitors (although in some cases, the savings to customers are sharply reduced when post and packaging is taken into account). In turn, the book retailers have been forced to set up their own internet operations, running the risk of cannibalising their own sales. This development may increase the sum of human wealth but not necessarily that of the corporate sector.

Working out the numbers

These grand theories are all very well. But analysts need numbers if they are actually going to say that internet company A is worth more or less than internet company B.

One valuation approach was a sort of variant on the line from the movie *Field of Dreams* – 'if you build it, he will come'. In this case, it was 'if you get them to come, they will buy something'. Provided you could get someone to look at your website, it was assumed you could earn some money out of them. So the key measure was 'eyeballs' – the number of page views of the site.

This kind of measure tells you something but not much. I look in a lot of shop windows when I walk down the high street but I don't tend to buy much. My occasional glances do not bring in any revenue.

Some companies based their valuation of the number of registered users of the site – those people who have bothered to fill in a form online. This was an advance on the 'shop window' principle, but not by much. People might easily register out of curiosity and then discover that the site was of little use to them. But even those who accepted site user numbers as a valid approach faced a further problem. The numbers did not always agree. Companies kept their own records of website visitors but outsiders often relied on panel surveys compiled by independent research groups. The former system, surprise, surprise, tended to produce higher numbers than the latter.

When you looked underneath the user numbers towards the number of paying customers, the story became rather different. When it floated on the stock market, Lastminute.com had 800,000 registered users. But only 29,000 people had actually made a purchase on the site. Its revenue over the year to 30 September 1999 was just £195,000. Lastminute.com's initial stock market valuation was thus around £19,000 for each of its 30,000 paying customers. Even if one assumed that its customer base increased tenfold to 300,000, that valuation would still equate to £1,900 per customer. Lastminute receives a commission (judged on its flotation figures) of around 7.5 per cent. So that valuation required each customer to spend around £25,000 on holidays, theatre tickets etc. over the course of their lifetime on the website. It was a pretty tall order.

Of course, valuation approaches based on eyeballs were not unprecedented. TV programmes are judged in terms of viewer numbers, because the greater the number of viewers, the easier it is to sell adverts. But that brings us back to an earlier problem – the effectiveness of internet advertising.

Another way to approach the internet valuation problem was to take the 'big picture' view. Investors would estimate the potential size of the market for the service, guess at the proportion of the market that would be captured by the company and come up with a value that way.

Take Freeserve, the internet service provider. Paul Gibbs, a valuation expert at the US investment bank J. P. Morgan, walked me through an assessment of this stock in March 2000, close to the peak of dotcom enthusiasm. He assumed that UK retail sales would grow at 4.8 per cent a year for the next seventeen years. He then assumed that online sales would capture 25 per cent of this total, that portals would get 50 per cent of online sales and that Freeserve would get 30 per cent of the portal market. If Freeserve could retain an 8 per cent commission on sales, that would mean revenues from e-commerce of £1.3bn by 2017. A similar set of assumptions led him to believe that Freeserve would get £1.2bn of advertising revenue by that date.

So a company with just £18m of sales in 2000 would have around £2.5bn by 2017. Take off 20 per cent for costs, discount those future revenues to allow for the time value of money and the result was a fair value for Freeserve shares of 649p. Mind you, at the time the share price of Freeserve was nearly 800p. If you consider that Mr Gibbs' assumptions were quite heroically bold, one has to wonder what those who paid 800p were expecting. (By April 2001, the company completed a merger with French ISP Wanadoo after the shares had slumped to below the original flotation price of 150p.)

But one has to suspect that sophisticated valuation methods of the kind used by Mr Gibbs were not at the heart of investors' decision-making in early 2000. When it floated, Freeserve was virtually the only pure internet play on the UK market. If you wanted to take a punt on the growth of the internet, you had to own it. There was not that much stock to own. Freeserve's parent company Dixons, the electrical goods retailer, retained an 80 per cent stake. So only 20 per cent of the company was available to the market.

The peculiar construction of stock market indices created additional demand for the stock. Only 20 per cent of Freeserve's shares might be tradable, but when it joined the market 100 per cent of its valuation was included in the FTSE All-Share index.[7] If you were an 'index-tracking' fund manager (someone who tries to match the performance of an index), you simply had to own the shares. Even if you were a traditional fund manager, you probably had to own them – if Freeserve shares shot up and you did not own them, you would underperform the rest of the industry. That would make it likely that you would lose business – clients would shift their money to a manager that had bought Freeserve.

In short, there was too much demand chasing too little supply. Prices shot up. This was a trick that was pulled off all over the world. In Germany, Deutsche Telekom floated just 10 per cent of its internet service provider T-Online. In the US, 3com floated a 6 per cent stake of its Palm hand-held computer business.

Floating off a stake in the subsidiary suited the parent companies very well. First of all, they raised some cash at an attractive valuation. Secondly, by getting a stock market quotation for the most exciting part of their business, they enhanced the valuation of the overall operation. Normally, a spin-off caused the shares of the parent company to rise. And, whilst doing all this, they retained control of the business.

The people who got the short end of the stick, of course, were investors. But perhaps it was their own fault. 'At a certain point of time, it became apparent that valuations were being set by supply and demand – in particular, a lack of supply – rather than some performance metric,' says Victor Basta of Broadview. 'People would say that "I can't get stock, I'd like to get stock ..." so the price would double.'

'As always there was an element of the Klondike,' says Richard Hunter of NatWest Stockbrokers. 'There was a great deal of unrealistic valuations of dotcom stocks.'

Two US authors did point to the absurdity of valuations at the time. In their book, *The Internet Bubble*, Anthony Perkins and Michael Perkins came up with a valuation system for dotcom stocks.[8] They assumed that net companies would grow their revenues by 65 per cent a year for five years, that future net margins would be 15 per cent and, at the end of the five-year period, the stocks would be awarded a price–earnings ratio of 40.

They then assumed that investors would demand a 20 per cent annual return from such stocks to compensate them for the higher risk. On that basis, the authors reckoned that most internet stocks were worth less than half their value as of mid 1999. And that was well below the peak.

Few listened to people like the Perkinses at the time. But what about the analysts we see quoted in the press or on TV? Why didn't they spot the problem and tell investors to buy the cheap stocks and sell the overvalued, frothy ones? Because that's not what they tend to do. According to analysis by Bloomberg, 63 per cent of all recommendations made by analysts are to buy a share, just 7.2 per cent are to sell. In the US, the figures are even more stark, 73.3 per cent buys and just 1.9 per cent sells. The worst label that an analyst will normally attach to a company's shares is something like 'market perform' (it will go up and down in line with everything else) or 'hold' (neither buy nor sell).

Analysts' reluctance to use the word 'sell' is quite understandable. Companies do not like it. They may refuse to speak to the analyst in future, making life very difficult for him or her. But an even bigger factor is that analysts work for investment banks, whose main source of profits is conducting deals for the corporate sector – organising takeovers, selling off subsidiaries, raising money via share or bond issues.

It will not help the investment bank get the business if the analyst has been negative about the company's shares. Indeed, the analysts are under great pressure to come up with lots of 'buy' ideas to help their corporate finance colleagues get a foot in the door with company executives. As a result, analysts are perennial optimists. 'Bottom up' analysts – those who look at individual companies – perennially have higher earnings forecasts than their 'top down' colleagues – who look at the overall economic position.

A classic bottom up approach is to compare one company in a sector with another. So one could argue that Ebahgum shares were cheap at £600 per registered user, compared with Eeitscold shares at £800 per user. This relative approach, of course, completely ignores the possibility that both company's shares might be massively overvalued.

Take Freeserve. A profile in *Sunday Business* newspaper in February 2000 revealed that not one of the sixteen brokers who followed the company had a 'sell' recommendation or something similar. At the time, Freeserve shares were between 700p and 800p. By October of that year, they were 160p.

Another hot stock was QXL.com, the internet auction house. In February 2000, Goldman Sachs, one of the most prestigious investment banks in the world, started coverage of the shares with a 'market outperform' recommendation. At the time, the shares were the equivalent of 350p. By April 2001, they were 5p. That is the definition of *under*performance.

It is not as if, in either case, the merits of the shares were unquestioned. Neither company was making a profit. Both faced competition from big US rivals, such as America Online or eBay. Both shares had shot up from their flotation price, respectively 150p for Freeserve and the equivalent of 50p for QXL.com.[9]

There was even one obvious oddity that should have prompted alarm bells. Freeserve was 80 per cent owned by the electrical retailer Dixons. At one point in early 2000, the market value of Dixons was less than the value of its stake in Freeserve. That suggested one of three possibilities: the shops owned by Dixons were worthless, Dixons shares were cheap or that Freeserve shares were too expensive.

So with all that evidence, you would have thought that at least one analyst would have gone against the crowd and advised investors to sell shares in Freeserve. But not one of sixteen experts made the right call. One habit, common in 1999 and 2000, was to set a 'price target' for a share and to set that target far above the current level. Henry Blodget, an internet analyst at Merrill Lynch, made his name by setting a price target of $400 a share, for Amazon.com in December 1998; the target was passed within months. Of course, the kind of investor sentiment prevailing at the time could make such prophecies self-fulfilling; if everyone believed the price would reach $400, they would be happy to buy at $200 or $300, thus pushing the price in the right direction.

Price target inflation set in. Setting a high target price for a share made the company happy, existing shareholders happy and made the analyst's reputation if the target was achieved. There was very little incentive to be circumspect.

There are very good analysts, of course, who make honest efforts to pore through accounts and uncover discrepancies. But their life can be a hard one. When one analyst, Terry Smith, wrote a book which criticised the accounts of many leading UK companies, he quickly lost his job.[10] And most of the commentators who did draw attention to some of the internet overvaluations in early 2000 tended to be dismissed as curmudgeons. They just didn't 'get it' because they were too narrowminded to grasp the potential of the internet. Warren Buffett, one of the great investors of all time, was regarded as a 'dinosaur' because he refused to invest in such stocks.

But the purchase of some of these stocks was, in effect, a game of musical chairs, with investors hoping to make a very quick profit before the music stopped. Someone would be left without a seat when the music stopped but every investor clearly thought it would not be them.

When these stocks fell, they were bound to fall by a lot. First of all, a large number of investors were 'momentum players', people who bought stocks because they were going up. When the shares stopped going up, those investors were no longer interested; their main aim was to get their money out as quickly as possible.

Secondly, technology stocks are 'long duration' assets. Much of their value consists of the expectation of future profits, discounted to the present day. A small change in those expectations, or a small increase in the discount rate used, has a big impact on the present value of the shares. This makes the stocks highly volatile.

Plenty of people must have bought at the peak and subsequently will have cursed their foolishness. As of 16 November 2000, sixty stocks in the All-Share had fallen more than 60 per cent since the 6 March peak in the Techmark and twenty-one had dropped by more than 80 per cent, the latter including some of the stocks most treasured by investors in the early months of the year: QXL.com, Thus, Durlacher, Scotia Holdings, Danka Business, DCS, Moneyextra, Infobank, Shaw (Arthur), Financial Objects, Kewill Systems, Atlantic Telecom, Vocalis, Freeserve, Kingston Communications, Bell Group, 365 Corporation, Cantab Pharmaceuticals, Easy Screen, Future Network and IMS.

Let us assume that the majority of those stocks will never reach their peaks again. (This is quite likely. If a stock falls by 80 per cent, it will have to rise fivefold to regain its former level.) There will thus have been a direct transfer of wealth between those who sold at the peak (or close to it) and those who bought.

You might say, I suppose, that all is fair in love and stock markets. Those who bought at the peak were either institutions (who can afford the loss) or private investors (who paid a price for their greed/ignorance.) In fact, some of the *FT* readers I polled seemed to have quite a sophisticated approach to the dotcom stocks. They were not just buying for the sake of it. Steve Bennetts bought shares in US group Amazon.com after the chief financial officer 'explained the model to me – briefly, the opportunity to build a large business from a relatively small asset base and also the dynamics of the cash cycle – essentially building the business by collecting cash from customers in one or two days and paying book wholesalers in fifty days.'

There also seemed to be a solid phalanx of investors who were unimpressed by dotcom stocks. Malwa Cotton ignored them – 'Many do not have a sustainable business model and those that do have inadequate cash flow' – although he did use websites to track financial news.

Joe Cittern said that 'I haven't invested in the likes of Lastminute, for example, because it was obvious they were overblown, and whilst there might have been money to be made, I didn't want to be the "greater fool" left holding the baby. I have invested in many hi-tech companies that many might regard as dotcoms but are in fact powering the wireless/internet wave rather than being froth on the top.'

Stephen Rivett bought shares in Interactive Investor and sold quickly at a handsome profit. 'Apart from that, I didn't invest in dotcom stocks – overvalued, trumped up and a farce – only a tiny few will ever make money.'

But some investors caught the bug. Liz Cameron invested in dotcom issues 'before the bubble burst, in order to make a lot of money in a short time'. She says her investment in Teamtalk.com was a disaster and she is now leaving dotcom stocks well alone. Another investor, who did not want to be named, said: 'I invested in Interactive, Lastminute and Stepstone [the recruitment agency]. I think I must have caught the TMT fever and I thought some quick money could be made. It comes down to greed, I guess, getting the better of me.'

James McCarthy invested in the website Interactive Investor International 'because I used their website and figured that the desire for financial information will increase in society as a whole. With Interactive Investor, the bulletin boards are a fun way of judging other people's sentiment and research (or lack of it). It's a small amount of money to risk but it does spice up my portfolio.' He adds that: 'I didn't invest in Lastminute.com or Stepstone, because I couldn't see any future for what they are doing. It's too easy to replicate.'

Some investors clearly realised that these companies might have little chance of success, but they saw their share prices were rising in leaps and bounds. Why should they miss out when everyone else was earning easy money?

'People were doing nothing more than gambling but they did so willingly,' says Jeremy King of ProShare. 'They knew they were having a punt but they did so knowingly. They felt it was a risk they were prepared to take.'

Of course, it is natural to think that the market is all-knowing, can price shares correctly and can spot the industrial titans of the future. But the market can get things spectacularly wrong. In the mid 1990s, biotechnology stocks were all the rage and the UK leader, British Biotech, looked set to join the FTSE 100 index. The company had a drug, marimastat, which promised to be a cure for one kind of cancer. That was an idea that had the same potential as the internet – just imagine the sales of a cancer cure round the globe.

But, of course, the market couldn't *know* whether the drug would work – it had to guess. And in the case of British Biotech, the market guessed wrong. Tests showed that marimastat was ineffective. British Biotech shares plunged.

Once one accepts the idea that the markets can be inefficient, then one can see the dangers in the kind of manias that marked late 1999 and early 2000. Good, solid profit-making companies can be denied capital or can find it more expensive to raise new money. Flaky companies can be funded which simply destroy wealth and damage the savings of individual investors.

Take the emerging markets boom of the early 1990s, when scarcely anybody had heard of the internet. The emerging markets story seemed genuinely compelling. Countries in south-east Asia, Latin America and eastern Europe were gradually adopting liberal capitalism. Their economies would naturally grow faster than those of western Europe or the US either because of more rapid population growth or because they had more catching up to do. That rapid economic growth would translate into faster profits growth and thus greater profits for equity investors.

In their day, emerging market funds were as popular as technology funds in early 2000. Institutions and private investors flocked to buy them. The result was a flood of hot money into the countries concerned. Some was used wisely; a lot was not. It is an old rule that when capital is plentiful, it tends to be squandered. Prestige property projects were built; countries created 'national champions' in industries where they had little prospect of profit; croneyism and corruption were rife.

The problems were swift to emerge. In December 1994, Mexico, having vowed never to do so, devalued the peso, causing heavy losses to investors in its bonds; the US stepped in with a rescue package. Ah well, said the Asian enthusiasts, Latin America has let down investors many times before. Asia is different. But in 1997, Thailand, struggling in the face of a massive trade deficit, devalued the baht and set off a wave of selling across Asian markets.

Once again, investors had proved far too optimistic. They had extrapolated the growth rates of Asian economies into infinity. They had ignored the region's problems. And in their exuberance, they had helped bring on the crash.

Note how the pattern is so familiar. An investment category becomes fashionable. Investors pile in. By doing so, they validate their own judgment by pushing up prices. That entices more buyers, and so on. But when the first bad news breaks, those wanting to sell find there is no one left to buy. That causes share prices to fall sharply, flushing out more sellers, and the downward spiral continues.

Valuing shares, or stock markets, is not a science but an art. Investors often make mistakes, erring on the side of overconfidence and extrapolation. That's why investing in the market is never easy money.

5

Career Options

We could see that the internet was coming and we had to be part of it.

Internet entrepreneur

I was offered a job in early 2000. It was very hard to resist. The salary was good but the main pitch from the headhunter concerned the share options. I was being offered options over the equivalent of 1 per cent of a dotcom company. At that time, many such companies were being floated on the stock market for £100m or more. The offer equated to what the headhunter called 'a seven figure opportunity'. It sounded like easy money. That's the beauty of share options. They can be scattered around like confetti. People like me could in theory become millionaires within months – if only we choose the right company.

I turned the job down. (At the time of writing, the company had not floated, so I would still be waiting for my millions.) At the time, a lot of my colleagues would have considered me stupid for doing so. Media was a hot area for internet recruitment in the late 1999/early 2000 period. Chris Price, an *FT* colleague who did eventually make the leap into the dotcom world, said he and a colleague were receiving around an offer a day in the first few months of the year.

And it was not just the media. Anyone with technology or management skills was seen as fair game for the headhunters. In the US, even top business schools like Harvard were finding that students were not finishing their courses but leaving to join internet start-ups.[1] It all made life very difficult for 'old economy' companies. Should they do nothing and lose some of their best employees? Or increase salaries to keep them, and risk a big rise in costs?

Some token measures were taken. There was some evidence that the informal style of dotcom life was attractive to some employees. 'Old economy' firms duly extended the right to wear casual dress from Fridays to the rest of the week – a move which had no revenue cost. (Pretty soon, it turned out that the term 'casual dress' was open to many different definitions. Ripped jeans and dirty T-shirts were out. What was wanted was the 'smart casual' dress that some nightclubs demand. As they gazed mournfully at their wardrobes, some male employees might have longed for the simplicity of the old suit rule.)

Some more tangible attractions were offered. In August 2000, Andersen Consulting, a management consultancy group, said that it would give its graduate recruits a signing-on bonus of £10,000 to offset competition from dotcom groups.

But there was no way that an old economy company could offer the same kind of options package as a dotcom. Only the top executives in an old economy company could hope to earn millions out of options. In a dotcom, even the lowliest members of staff could in theory do so.

Such a transformation would not have been possible twenty years ago when I left college. Most of my middle-class friends joined the professions – accountancy, the law, chartered surveying, the Civil Service. Few thought of joining a business – the idea was totally unappealing. Not only did the thought of preparing production schedules seem achingly boring, management in Britain appeared to consist of an endless round of confrontations with trade unions. Who needed the hassle?

Small businesses, in particular, were for the birds. They were either family companies (what in the US are called Mom'n'Pop operations) where, if you weren't part of the family, you were always a second-class citizen. Or else they were fragile enterprises that could offer none of the security we craved – few holidays and no pension.

And as for the idea of starting your own business, forget it. It would be hard to raise the money. It would be a twenty-four-hour job. And we had no bright ideas.

With the right application, however, a life in the professions would be ultimately comfortable. After ten years or so, you would become a partner in your law or accountancy firm and then the money would start to roll in.

You would not be rich in your twenties but you had a good chance of being so in your forties.

Working for a partnership was the most likely road to wealth. There were no such things as share options in those days and industrial pay, even for senior managers, was modest by today's standards – executives had to worry about what their workers might think. A partnership, in contrast, could pay its senior staff handsomely without the tiresome glare of publicity.

Nowadays, security seems a much less valued concept. Perhaps employees have realised, after years of downsizing and re-engineering, that very few employers can actually deliver it. A small, even unknown, business may have exactly the same downside in terms of security as a large corporation – but it will offer a lot more upside.

And working for a small business, particularly in the dotcom world, can simply be more exciting. Take Ajaz Ahmed, who dropped out of Bath University, where he was studying business, to start the consultancy AKQA with three friends. 'We could see that the revolution was coming and we had to be part of it. If I waited to finish my degree, I might have missed the moment. We knew the internet was as important as the personal computer revolution.'

Or Rob Golding, a former stock market analyst who works for a technology publishing company Tornado-Insider.com. 'The great joy of it is that I am working with so many like-minded people who want to be involved in a changing world. To miss it and sit at home and watch it would just be terrible. A common thread in my life for twenty-five years had been the motor industry and, although it is an exciting high-risk industry, at the financial level, it's very depressing. No matter what they do, managers never seem to add value.' To Golding, the Tornado project 'seemed like the new world to someone mired in the old world'.

Of course, the opportunity to join a new company depends on that company being created in the first place. And that is where the venture capital industry comes in. The US has had a flourishing venture capital industry for decades. The VCs, as they are dubbed, have been more than willing to fund start-ups in the technology industry – indeed, some attribute the success of the US economy to this factor.

In the UK, venture capitalists have traditionally tended to focus on management buyouts of existing companies – backing the incumbent management of a quoted company, or a quoted company's subsidiary. The theory is that managers will run the business more effectively if they are given a substantial equity stake. That is a less risky business than backing start-ups. But in recent years, US venture capitalists have come to Europe looking for new opportunities – and that has prompted the domestic VCs to respond to the competition. It has become much easier for start-ups to get funded.

Robert Norton came up with the idea for a Europe-wide natural health and beauty products group in March 1999. In June, he quit his job as a business development director at Nomad, a French dotcom group. Together with partner Toby Rowland, he founded Clickmango in August 1999, and then raised £3m from Atlas Ventures and Jacob Rothschild within just eight days, one of the fastest capital-raising exercises yet recorded.

Not only was this a remarkably rapid deal, it was also a more substantial fund-raising for a start-up than had been seen before. 'At the time it was quite a large step up in funding, since QXL and Lastminute had only raised £1m or so in the first round,' recalls Norton. Normally, venture capitalists put in only small amounts of capital at the 'seed money' stage, simply to allow the company to get established. Only when the company starts operating, and looks like being successful, do substantial sums roll in.

Norton and Rowland retained substantial stakes in the business and, simply by getting substantial funding, they had in theory become wealthy. 'On paper we were millionaires and I suddenly found myself on the *Sunday Times* list of rich people under thirty,' recalls Norton. But in fact both he and partner Toby Rowland found their lifestyles downgraded by the move. 'I left behind substantial amounts of stock options when I left Nomad,' he says. 'Both of us took a large salary cut and I was sleeping on a blow-up mattress for months.'

Norton and Rowland came up with their own business plan and so at least had some control over their futures. The humble employee joining a dotcom has no such control but has to be equally careful about choosing the right company. Chris Price rejected the offers he received from B2C (business-to-consumer) companies that were at a variety of levels, from business development, through financial communications to marketing director. 'I wasn't convinced in the business model – there was obvious overheating around that period. And I wasn't going to leave the *FT* unless I was going to have fun. You have to think about the business you're going to go to,' says Price. 'I never believed that a stand-alone media site would work. Those sites are now looking for a second round of funding and it's not forthcoming.'

Eventually, Price was approached by Mike Whittaker of NewMedia-SPARK, a company quoted on the Alternative Investment Market. He was starting a company called EONet, having previously founded Collins Stewart, the broker. 'When he told me about the business, which was offering private investors the chance to put money in pre-IPO [initial public offering] stocks, I thought this was an absolute killer of an idea,' says Price. 'My job would be as content director with the aim of designing and building a new website which would be "sticky" – keep investors on the site. I was given options over 1 per cent of the company and a nice increase in salary.'

Rob Golding says he, too, was choosy when it came to taking the dotcom plunge. Tornado's founder, Dutch businessman Jerome Mol, had just sold his software company to Hewlett-Packard and Golding 'felt it was unlikely we would exhaust his resources within a few months'.

Ajaz Ahmed entered the industry in its early phase, when the internet was little known. He did not have the luxury afforded to those who founded companies in 1999, when venture capitalists gathered around entrepreneurs like moths round a nightlight. 'Every bank said no when we asked for finance; in fact everyone said no,' he recalls. Luckily, Ahmed had personally accumulated shares in Microsoft, Apple, Intel and Motorola, and he sold those to finance the business.

He and his friends chose a name based on initials rather than go for the dotcom moniker. 'A lot of businesses founded at that time had funky names based on web or net but we wanted to be able to evolve the business as we wanted,' he recalls. (A sensible move. At some time, all those names beginning with e- or mixing upper and lower case letters in some absurd combination are going to look terribly dated.)

AKQA is a consultancy, advising companies on how to deal with the new economy. 'We started off in digital TV, and have moved on to the net and to PDAs [personal digital assistants],' says Ahmed. The group now has clients such as Nike, Microsoft, BMW, Sainsbury and Lloyds TSB.

'The critical thing we did was that we helped define the marketplace,' Ahmed recalls. 'We took out full page advertisements in the trade press and made people want to buy our service.' The strategy had almost instant success. The first client was Coca-Cola (GB), which came after just a month.

Lack of finance meant he could not afford to go on a Boo.com-style spending spree. 'When you don't have the option of refunding, you have to be profitable from day one.' But Ahmed's gamble paid off. Soon he was turning down money. 'Once we started getting headlines in the trade press, lots of people were calling us, wanting to invest, but it was very difficult to see what value they'd add.'

AKQA now employs 150 people, and the group has moved from its initial premises in Ascot to fashionable Jermyn Street in the West End where its offices sit between those of management consultants McKinsey and *The Economist* (and next to the nightclub Tramp). Ahmed's company was only one of thousands set up in the late 1990s. The beauty of this period was that everyone was feeling their way. The internet would, in theory, change almost every aspect of business and personal life. Who could tell which businesses could succeed and which would not? Venture capitalists were not sure, nor were private investors. So if you wanted to set up your own business, this was the perfect time to try it. Money was available to fund your dreams.

The dotcom working life

Ahmed's only job has been at AKQA, so the informality of dotcom life is all he has known. For Price and Golding, both of whom have worked for big organisations in the past, life in the dotcom world has seen a big shift in working culture. 'Decisions get made much more quickly,' says Price. 'And I get respect from my fellow directors. It is invigorating, using different skill sets.'

'It's a real rollercoaster, I've worked an awful lot harder than I planned to at this stage of my career,' says Golding. 'It's quite difficult to adjust to the chaos implicit in a start-up company. If you hire someone, there's no personnel manager, if the IT crashes, there may be no one around to fix it.'

The lack of support can be quite disconcerting to someone used to working in a more structured environment. And working for any kind of start-up business generally involves a lot of hard work. The public image of dotcom life was rather false. There was lots of talk of free soft drinks and an informal atmosphere. But in fact the hours were long, as employees struggled to play a multiplicity of roles. Everything had to be built from scratch – the technology, the brand name, the sales staff, even the product itself. Those free soft drinks were on offer to keep employees happy during the long working nights – after all, they often had no time to get to a store to buy their own drinks.

A survey[2] of 220 graduates from the London Business School and the IESE Business School in Barcelona found that, as reality sank in, the lure of dotcoms was fading. According to the report, 'Our study explodes the general consensus that dotcoms offer a better quality of life and a more fun environment. The hours worked are longer, the travel is more onerous and time at home is limited. The new economy company increasingly mirrors the old, but without a supportive infrastructure.' The survey found that 48 per cent of e-company executives worked more than sixty hours a week, compared with 38 per cent of other respondents. Forty per cent spend ten or more nights away from home a month compared with 16 per cent of the others.

To make matters worse the collapse in technology share prices that began in March 2000 removed a significant incentive for joining a dotcom business. Not only might the job not create millions, it might not last for very long. A friend of mine, a Harvard MBA, worked without pay for some months at one struggling US dotcom, as the executives attempted to turn the business round.

Rob Golding recalls the period 'I joined [Tornado-Insider] at Christmas 1999; within a few days I was worth three times my "in" price. But in the second quarter, when the tech boom started going into reverse, I stopped doing sums based on the value of my equity.'

'The atmosphere when I joined in March was that nothing was going to stop this thing,' says Chris Price. 'Now, seven months later,[3] the wheels have fallen off the dotcom bandwagon. That has big ramifications as a worker. There is more stress. But it also forces you to take a longer-term view of how you're going to do this.'

Ahmed also thinks that life has changed in the wake of the sector's share-price declines. 'I regularly get e-mails from students and I advise them to finish their degrees. The circumstances when we started AKQA were quite different.'

When he was interviewed for this book Chris Price was still optimistic about his prospects for a big pay-off at EONet. 'When I was first approached, the job, the salary and the options were all equally attractive but if you asked me now, I'd say the options. In normal life, what were the chances of someone like me netting a million pounds?'

Price reckons EONet will survive the dotcom shakeout. 'Our business is not entirely internet-dependent and the calibre of management is senior executives from investment banking.' And he feels the dotcom era has been incredibly positive. 'I hope what has happened [the share price falls in tech stocks] won't kill the entrepreneurial spirit.' Alas, after the interview was conducted and while this book was being edited, Chris left EONet and is now working as a journalist again.

Robert Norton of Clickmango has certainly not lost his entrepreneurial drive despite the failure of his company. When I spoke to him in December 2000, he was still talking with Atlas Ventures about further business opportunities. Looking back on Clickmango, Norton says: 'I feel tremendously rewarded that we were given the opportunity to start the business in the first place. I always wanted to run my own business and you either learn through great success or failure.' He says that while his business was funded incredibly quickly, the set-up period was too long. 'We got the money in September but we didn't launch until April, spent seven months sorting out the site.' By the end of that time, the Nasdaq market in the US had fallen sharply, and in terms of funding at least, Clickmango had missed the boat.

Easy option

Share options are at the heart of dotcom culture but it is hard sometimes to remember why executive options were introduced in the first place. They were seen as the answer to a problem – what one might call the 'expense account' lifestyle.

In the 1980s, being a senior manager at a big US corporation was seen as a licence to spend money. Chauffeured limos, first-class air travel, lunches at the best restaurants – all were seen as legitimate perks of the job. The US corporate sector appeared to be falling behind the Japanese – the reasons were many, but one appeared to be that US executives were too busy getting their snouts in the trough.

What was the answer? The cause of the problem, critics asserted, was that the management and ownership of companies had become divorced. Managers had no significant stake in the companies they ran; share ownership was concentrated in the hands of faceless institutions. The only way to bridge the gap was to align the interests of the two by making managers part owners of the business. Specifically, they needed to be given share options. That way, managers would make money when shareholders made money.

Nowadays, share options are seen as one of the cornerstones of liberal capitalism. By giving workers a stake in the business, they break down the barriers between capital and labour. From the manager's point of view, they encourage employee loyalty and ensure that at least part of an employee's compensation is tied to the success of the business. They have also made many executives (especially in the US) extremely rich.

From an employee's point of view, share options seem like free money. A few have been made millionaires. Many more have made thousands or tens of thousands of pounds – enough to pay for a holiday or repay the mortgage. (I should declare that I have benefited from the share option scheme run by Pearson, the owners of the *Financial Times*.)

The profits earned by employees from share options have been enhanced by the government's favourable tax treatment. Many ordinary UK employees will have acquired their shares through what are known as SAYE (save as you earn) schemes. Employees put aside up to £250 a month from their salaries. At the end of a three-, five- or seven-year period, interest will be added and the money accumulated used to buy shares at a discounted price (normally 20 per cent below the market price at the start of the saving period). Any profit is free from income tax, although not from capital gains tax.

Shares can also be accumulated though profit-sharing schemes, in which employees are given free stock provided certain financial targets are met. As long as the shares are held for three years, the proceeds are free of income tax.

At the time of writing, the government was also instituting a third, even more generous scheme. Employees will be able to save money out of pre-tax income – in other words, their contributions will be tax-deductible. Employers will also be able to match their contributions, that is, double them. So if you are a 40 per cent taxpayer, a £60 monthly contribution could buy you £200 worth of shares.

By 1997–8, some £16bn of shares (at the option price value) were owned through employee SAYE schemes and £4.8bn through profit-share schemes. A further £19bn was in so-called discretionary schemes, which are more skewed towards executives. Among big companies, these schemes were very common; 93 per cent of Footsie companies had SAYE schemes and 65 per cent profit-sharing schemes.

Many high-ranking employees would now not even consider moving to a new company unless share options were part of the package. For a young dotcom company, they represented the main reason to join. It is easy to see why dotcom companies were so eager to hand options out. If the options made the employee rich, then great – that would mean the founders and original investors would also have become wealthy. And if the options expired worthless, it would be bad news – but at least the options were always just paper. No cash had changed hands.

What is wrong with this generosity? Well, one could make the point that the tax benefits represent a transfer of wealth to those people who work for companies quoted on the stock market from those who do not – anyone who works for the public sector, or a charity, or a small business (you can, of course, be given shares in an unquoted business but this is normally only a lucrative benefit if the company subsequently floats on the market). So not only do the likes of nurses and teachers have to put up with lower pay than people in the private sector, they also have no chance of a lucrative options windfall. What's wrong with that? One could argue that it is the private sector that employs the 'wealth creators', whereas the public sector simply consumes wealth, so the former should be given greater incentives. On the other hand, the private sector would not get very far if the British population was permanently sick, or could not read or write.

Aside from these social or moral issues, there is the more important question of whether share option schemes achieve their stated purpose. Do they encourage or reward greater employee effort? The answer is not as obvious as you might think.

One of my best friends is a partner in a chartered surveying firm and he is quite clear that he feels greater commitment because the company is 'his' business. In his case, there is an obvious link between the decisions he takes and the clients he recruits, through to the success of the business and his own pay. Similarly, in writing this book, the fact that I am receiving a royalty gives me a great incentive to make it as readable and interesting as possible – and its success or failure is largely down to my efforts.

But does the average employee of, say, Ford, really feel that his or her efforts make the slightest bit of difference to the overall success of the company? In such huge and diverse companies, the answer must surely be no. One management mistake or a fire at a factory or a faulty component can offset the efforts of many thousands of workers.

I suppose you could argue that share-owning workers are less likely to go on strike. But the number of strikes has fallen for many reasons, including the decline of both union power and of manufacturing industry, the growth of part-time and female labour and changes to government legislation. Share ownership has probably played only a modest part in the decline.

There is, undoubtedly, a loyalty benefit to companies that flows from the lock-in provisions of share saving schemes. A worker who knows that he or she is about to make a healthy profit from his share options is less likely to quit for a competitor. Workers who leave before the end of a SAYE scheme get their cash back (with some interest), not shares. But, of course, such loyalty effects last only as long as the lock-in period. Once you have the shares, rather than just the options, you will suffer no financial loss by leaving. And this loyalty effect depends crucially on the ability of the share price to keep rising, a point I'll return to in a minute.

Just as crucially, the interests of workers and shareholders can be in conflict. Some businesses – mobile phones, technology infrastructure – have such good long-term growth prospects that they will tend to take on more workers as time goes on. The rising tide will lift all boats.

But for many more established businesses, growing sales and profits is hard work. In manufacturing industry, the only way to increase profits is to cut costs. And the biggest cost of all tends to be labour. The only way for one worker to see his shares grow in value may be for a fellow worker to lose his job. And for most employees, share option profits will be much smaller than annual wages. Continual rounds of redundancies might push up the share price, but they are likely to do nothing for worker morale.

This brings me to another problem with employee share option schemes. Not only do workers receive their annual *income* from a company, option schemes also mean they have a significant part of their *savings* in the company. All their eggs and their bacon are in one basket. If the company gets into trouble, they will see their savings decline in value at just the time they are most likely to lose their job.

Shares are a risky investment. In essence, they are a claim on the assets and profits of a company when all other claims have been met – from the taxman, from lenders, from suppliers and from employees. These claims tend to be fixed. If the business is going well, then the company will have more than enough money to meet them – and shareholders can claim the surplus. But if the business is going badly, then there may not be much, if anything, left when the other claimants have had their fill.

That is why most experts agree that, for small investors, the best way to invest in equities is via a diversified fund. Individual companies may get in trouble and go bust, but the entire corporate sector will not do so. By encouraging workers to concentrate their savings in the shares of their employer the tax system encourages employees to pursue a highly risky savings strategy.

We have not heard many complaints about this for the simple reason that most shares have gone up in recent years. This bull market has been fuelled by a lot of factors, as I have already described, including lower inflation and low interest rates. But while a bull market has made share options both profitable and popular, it has undermined part of the logic for their existence. The reason that employees have made so much money out of share options has been almost nothing to do with their effort and enthusiasm, but with changes in economic and monetary policy. When the stock market fell in 2000, it was not because UK employees had suddenly started to work less hard – it was because of a variety of factors, such as a fall on Wall Street, the bursting of the dotcom bubble and a slowing global economy.

In short, in big companies, an individual worker can have little impact on the success of the entire enterprise. And even if the business is successful, that might have no impact on the share price.

An end to the long bull market might also prove a nasty shock. In the twentieth century, around one in three years saw a fall in UK share prices – but there were none in the 1980s and only two in the 1990s.[4] The law of averages appeared to reassert itself in the course of 2000. In the past, there have been a number of five-year periods in which share prices have retreated. What price share options as an incentive when the share price is falling?

In the US, where share options are even more widely used than in the UK, there is an uneasy symbiosis between economic success, options and the stock market. When a company grants share options to an employee, it is obviously incurring a 'cost' – it is granting some part of its future value to an individual. That value will no longer be available to other investors. But companies are not required to charge this cost against their profits. As the great US investor Warren Buffett has written: 'If options aren't a form of compensation, what are they? If compensation isn't an expense, what is it? And if expenses shouldn't go in the calculation of earnings, where in the world should they go?'

Andrew Smithers, of the investment consultancy, Smithers & Co, has estimated that US corporate profits may have been overestimated by as much as a third because of the share option effect. To add to the distortion, when US employees exercise their options, they face a tax charge. The *employer* gets a tax rebate to offset that charge. So the company's tax bill is lower and its after-tax profits are higher as a result. In some cases, this rebate can be so large that the company pays no tax at all for a year. In October 2000, an analysis by an accountancy professor in *Barron's* weekly found that Cisco, one of the biggest companies in the world, would be loss-making if it charged the cost of granting options against profits.

This is a gravy train which no one wants to halt. So there is every temptation to keep the whole vehicle moving in the right direction. Companies have learned that the stock market punishes them, by sending the share price down sharply, if they fail to meet profit forecasts. So they make every effort to massage those forecasts and to manipulate the earnings numbers to ensure they are met – a special credit here, a pension refund there, whatever it takes to keep the analysts happy. After all, the wealth of the management and of the employees depends on it.

When there is such a great incentive to fiddle the numbers, the line between creative accounting and fraud is very thin. But even without fraud, the potential for share options to create a conflict of interest between management and investors is still there. A nice irony, given that option schemes were designed to ensure that the interests of managers and investors were aligned.

The problem is that options are a one-way bet. If the share price goes up, the management makes out like bandits. If it goes down, they don't lose any money – they just don't make any. OK, they could lose their jobs – but top managers these days tend to have very good severance packages, sometimes receiving the equivalent of three years' pay (not to mention pensions, health benefits and the rest).

Under option pricing theory, developed by professors Black and Scholes,[5] an option is most valuable when the underlying price is most volatile. Say you have options to buy shares in two companies at 150p, and the current price is 100p. But company A's price tends to double or halve every year, whereas company B's price varies by only 5 per cent or so. The option in company A is obviously more valuable, since it might be worth exercising this year; it will be more than ten years before there is much chance of a profit out of company B.

Why would a share price be volatile? The most likely reason is if the company is involved in a risky enterprise, such as diamond mining. So, if you are a manager, share options encourage you to take greater risks. If they come off, great, you're a millionaire – if they don't, you haven't made any money, but outside investors can pick up the tab.

One example of the way that managers are encouraged to take greater risks is the share buy-back. Under a buy-back, companies spend money to purchase their own shares in the market. The normal result is to increase earnings per share, one of the key measures of corporate achievement (this is because roughly the same amount of corporate profits is spread between a smaller number of shares). This boosts the share price in two ways. First, investors are aware that the company will be a steady buyer of shares – there is more demand and less supply. Second, investors are attracted to companies with high earnings per share growth. A virtuous circle can be created.

There is nothing intrinsically wrong with buy-backs. In principle, they are simply a means for companies to return cash to shareholders. Most experts would agree that, if companies have excess cash, they should hand it back to investors so they can use it more profitably elsewhere. Traditionally, the vehicle for returning cash was the dividend but in the US (and more recently in the UK), dividends have had an adverse tax treatment. Share buy-backs are given a more friendly treatment by the taxman.

Like many things, however, buy-backs are best enjoyed in moderation. After all, what is a company really saying when it buys back its own shares? In short, it is saying that it does not have sufficient profitable business opportunities to invest in. If that is the case, should investors really want to buy the company's shares? And how come so many companies are saying that the best use of their money is to buy their own shares? Isn't the world supposed to be enjoying a 'new era'? Aren't stocks trading at historically high ratings, supposedly because of the potential for rapid profits growth?

It can, of course, be seen as a sign of confidence that companies are buying their own shares (it certainly is seen as such when directors use *their own money* to do so). If the company is buying, outside investors could argue, it must be because the management thinks the price is going higher. But what if the managers are wrong?

In many cases, companies have gone far beyond using up spare cash to buy shares. They are actually borrowing money to do so. This is because current corporate finance theory argues that balance sheets are more 'efficient' when they have less equity and more debt. Interest on debt is tax-deductible whereas the dividends paid to shareholders are not. In addition, the requirement to meet regular debt payments imposes a discipline on managements and forces them to focus on generating cash.

Again, this theory is all very well up to a point. Incurring more debt makes a company more risky. Interest on debt has to be paid and the capital repaid, whereas dividends can be cut or eliminated and shareholders never get their equity back (from the company, that is – they can always sell their stake to other investors). This is all very well in boom times, such as we have enjoyed for much of the 1980s and 1990s, but in recessions, companies are usually glad to have as little debt as possible. Cash is king.

Share buy-backs prop up the share price in the short term and help managers make money from their options (indeed, arguably they are using the company's money to buy back shares with one hand while issuing shares to themselves with the other). But let us suppose, for a moment, that the stock market was flat, or fell, for a considerable time. What would happen? The workers and executives would suddenly find that their options were valueless. If the options truly acted as an incentive to better effort, their work would presumably suffer. Many would demand cash as a substitute. This cash demand would come at a tricky time. Any stock market setback would presumably be linked to economic difficulties, the kind of difficulties that tend to squeeze profit margins. In the US, corporate tax bills would rise as workers ceased to exercise their (now worthless) share options. The virtuous circle might become a vicious one.

There were already some signs of this in late 2000 and early 2001. A report from Hay Management Consultants found that e-businesses were planning to give their workers pay rises that were more than double the national average – in order to hang on to their staff. Share options were no longer cutting the mustard as an incentive.[6]

I am not saying that share options are a force for evil. All I am saying is that, after such a long bull market, it has been presumed that options are 'easy money'. As with so many examples in this book, the lure of easy money has its dangers. The widespread use of options has led managements to bend the rules. For example, if the share price falls sharply, it has been known for the option price to be changed so that everyone can cash in; a sort of heads we win, tails you lose for the modern era. (In October 2000, Sprint, the US telecoms company, repriced the options it had granted to 24,000 employees, after its shares had fallen 70 per cent from their high. The move was needed, said Sprint, to prevent a 'brain drain' of employees to other companies.) In March 2001, a UK dotcom company called InterX proposed a similar scheme, in the face of considerable opposition from outside shareholders.

Who indeed are the losers from this process? One group is the public sector workers that I mentioned earlier. But another is the external investors in the company. These largely consist of pension funds, insurance companies and the like – which represent the collective savings of millions of individuals.

But surely the external investors aren't fools? They can make their own assessment of the value of a company and if they think the odds are stacked against them, they can avoid the shares.

As we saw in Chapter 4, however, it's not quite as easy as that. Investors are not always rational and professional fund managers are being judged against their rivals. In theory, they are trying to build their clients' savings over the long term; in practice, they risk losing business if they underperform over a year, or even three months. They almost had to buy shares in dotcom companies if they were large enough. And generous share option schemes were so widespread that investors had very little choice. As fast as company insiders exercised their options and sold their shares, outsiders were scrambling to buy them. It will be interesting to see if a bear market changes the attitudes of employees and investing institutions towards the share option phenomenon.

6

Taking a Punt

For some people it's embarrassing to lose money. With the internet, they don't have to lose face by speaking to someone on the phone.

Bookmaker

Wander into the offices of a spread betting firm like Cantor Fitzgerald and you will come across a world far removed from the high street bookie's shop. No old men huddled over the *Racing Post*; no stubby pens; no furtive smokers frittering away their weekly wages. This is a high-class, high-tech operation that could pass for the dealing room of a bank. Spread betting is about serious people and serious money.

In early 2000, wire services carried stories about an unnamed spread better who had made a rapid £1m by gambling on the financial markets. Some of my colleagues at the *FT* set out to discover the gambler's identity, but their efforts were in vain; the betting companies are pretty discreet at protecting the identity of their clients. The story faded away again.

What I did find out, however, when having lunch with a senior gambling executive a few months later, was that the gambler had lost all that £1m again in the next few months.

Later on I had lunch with a doctor who was one of the best clients of one of the big spread betting firms. He had won, lost and won again £2m by speculating on the financial markets. Second time around, he was smart – while he continued to gamble, he bought himself a plane and a nice house with his winnings and limited the amount of capital he now devoted to speculation.

A spread bet requires the gambler to estimate whether a number will come out higher or lower than a certain range – the spread. That figure could be anything, from the number of throw-ins during a Premier League match to the seats won by the Conservatives at the next general election to the level of the FTSE 100 index.

The big difference from a traditional bet is that the amount you can win *and lose* varies enormously. You bet a certain amount per point, say £15. Let us say that when Brian Lara comes out to bat for the West Indies, you think he is going to score a lot of runs. The spread is 40–44. You think he is going to score more than 44 so you place an up bet at £15 a run (I saw somebody actually make this bet at Lord's). For every run that Brian scores above 44, you get £15. So if he gets 100, you get 56 times £15 or £840. But for every run he falls short of 44, you lose £15. If he is run out without facing a ball, for example, you would be out of pocket to the tune of £660. If you are pessimistic about Lara's chances, you can simply make a down bet. Here the key number is the bottom of the spread – 40. For every run he falls short of 40, you make £15; for every run, he exceeds it, you lose the same amount.

Fortunately, you do not have to watch frozen in horror if, after making a down bet, Lara beats his world record of 501. You can lock in your profits or losses by making the reverse bet. In the match I saw, Lara quickly advanced to 20 and the spread moved up to 60–65 or so. The gambler made a down bet at the new total. Now he had secured his profit. If Lara was out for 20, he would lose on his up bet to the tune of £360 (24 times £15) but he would gain £600 on his down bet (40 times £15). If Lara were out for 70, he would make £390 on his up bet but lose £150 on his down bet. However the numbers fell, the gambler had a profit of £240.

These are clearly serious amounts of money to bet on a game as unpredictable as cricket. And when betting on the financial markets, it is easy for the gains and losses to mount up to thousands of pounds. The Dow Jones Industrial Average has experienced two one-day falls of more than 500 points – so even if you were betting just £1 a point, you would have lost £500 in a matter of eight hours.

But, of course, those looking to make easy money do not focus too much on the potential for huge losses. It is the big gains they care about.

On the financial markets, you can bet on almost anything you care to name these days – individual share prices, stock market indices, currency movements, commodities, interest rates. The bookmakers are also quick to come up with 'novelty bets' on political or cultural events. The *Big Brother* show on Channel 4 attracted a lot of spread bets with viewers taking a gamble on the percentage vote received by each of the last three contestants.

As the spread betting companies are very keen to point out, any profits you make from your gambles are tax-free. There is gambling duty to pay but that cost is allowed for within the bookmaker's spread. If you come out ahead, you will not pay either income or capital gains tax, which is a distinct advantage over people who invest in the stock market directly.

A moment's thought, however, explains why this tax loophole exists. If gamblers were raking in millions of profits, the government would be sure to find a way to tax them. The reason that there is no tax is that, on average, there is no profit. For every gambler who makes money on an up bet, there is one who is losing by betting down. Indeed, a survey by consultants KPMG found that losers outnumbered winners among spread betters by around five to three.

The preponderance of losers is due to the spread. For the bookmaker, this works rather like the zero on a roulette wheel. A certain proportion of bets always fall within the spread, so that the gamblers lose money whether they made an up or a down bet.

The bookmakers will tell you that, from their point of view, making money from sports is a tricky proposition. They can get things spectacularly wrong, as they did during the 1999 cricket World Cup when they vastly underestimated the likely number of wides that would be delivered. There is also the possibility of fraud; the companies quickly stopped taking bets on the time of the first throw-in during a soccer match after balls were mysteriously hoofed into the stands straight from the kick-off.

Stuart Wheeler, chairman and chief executive of IG Index, the number one firm in the market, says that 'Some people are more apt to win at sport. There is no underlying market to set prices and at any time we are quoting 500. Someone calmly sitting at home and analysing the situation carefully can spot when our prices are wrong. One client has spotted that gamblers tend to overestimate the number of bookings in a match. When they have forced up the price, he tends to move in and sell the spread.'

When he talks of an 'underlying market' Wheeler is comparing sports with the financial markets. If you take a bet on, say, a rise in the shares of Marks & Spencer, the spread betting firm can hedge that bet elsewhere. If you bet that M&S shares will rise, the firm can cover itself by speculating that the price will fall. That's because there are lots of firms in the financial markets making those kinds of gambles every day. For sports, however, there are the bookmakers and no one else.

Wheeler is not your average bookmaker. A courteous old Etonian and army veteran, he has the manner of a venerable head of a firm of solicitors. He founded IG Index in 1975 to allow investors to speculate on the price of gold. The business grew slowly at first – bets on stock market indices only became available in 1981 after stock index futures were introduced in the US. The business floated on the stock market in 2000 and made Wheeler rich enough to make his own gamble – promising £5m, the largest recorded political donation in the UK, to help the Conservative Party early in 2001.

As an old hand in the business, Wheeler has seen it all. One client turned £32,000 into a million by making sixty-two successive winning bets on the price of commodities. Back at the time of the stock market crash of 1987, one IG client made over £500,000 by betting the market would fall, while another lost £800,000 betting the other way.

Wheeler says few gamblers are smart enough to walk away with the bulk of their winnings. One who did was the doctor I have already described. He had started getting interested in the stock market after he left medical school. He used all his savings to buy shares in British Aerospace on the basis of a *Sunday Times* newspaper tip. It turned out to be one of the best performing shares of the year.

He then discovered spread betting. During the 1995–8 bull run, he made a lot of money by backing the trend in the FTSE 100 and Dow Jones Industrial Average. But he got overconfident in 1998. He made £2m in the first six months of the year and then lost it all. (In the summer of 1998, the market was hit by a debt crisis in Russia and the near-collapse of Long-Term Capital Management, a US hedge fund.)

The FTSE 100 suddenly plunged to 4,600 and he felt 'stupid' about losing all the money he had gained. His nerve held and he kept his positions in place. Alan Greenspan, the chairman of the US Federal Reserve, suddenly cut interest rates and he was saved. The market climbed out of its funk and the Footsie was quickly back above 6,000. 'I was lucky,' the doctor admits.

By this stage, he was writing options – giving other people the right to buy or sell the index at a certain price. In return, the option writer gets a premium (like an insurance premium) that will be a pure profit if the option is not exercised. At the time we met, the FTSE 100 index was trading at 6,100 and he had written an option giving investors the right to sell him the index at 5,100. Unless the index fell heavily he would make money. But a crash would cost him dear.

Such high stakes are not unusual in the spread betting market. It tends to attract the high rollers. IG Index says it will take bets of £500 a point on the Dow or the Footsie during market hours. Given that the Footsie can quite often move 100 points in a day, that's a potential loss of £50,000 in a day.

With such high stakes, bad debts are a potential problem. In 1987, the firm was unsuccessful at reclaiming a debt of more than £100,000 from one client. 'We tend to budget 4.5 per cent of our trading revenues for bad debts,' says Wheeler. 'More often than not, it's less than that.' But spread betting firms have a great advantage over conventional bookmakers – their bets are enforceable in law. 'We do get the money back, but litigation is costly,' admits Wheeler.

Another advantage is that, if a bet starts to move against a client, the spread betting firm can ask him or her for extra money. Not answering the phone is no defence. 'If we can't get hold of a client and their position is losing money, we are entitled to close out the bet,' says Wheeler.

One man who ran into a bad debt problem with a spread betting firm was Jonathan Ainsley, whom I met in the autumn of 1999. He went thirteen times over his credit limit after a bad bet on the FTSE 100 and it took him four years to repay his debts. Remarkably enough, he wasn't put off the whole idea of gambling. He returned to spread betting and made £250,000 in one day when the US stock market suddenly plunged in August 1999.

Spread betting is, in effect, a version of one of the oldest games in the book – investing on margin. The latter was commonplace in the 1920s, when it was known for US investors to put down just 10 per cent of the price of a stock. In other words, with just £1,000 of capital, they could control £10,000 worth of shares.

Investing on margin works extremely well when stock markets are rising fast. An investor with 10 per cent margin will double his or her money if the share price goes up 10 per cent. If it goes down 10 per cent, however, they will lose all their initial investment. And if it falls 20 per cent, they will be required to put up more money – which they may or may not have.

To be fair to the spread betting firms, they try hard to avoid the obvious pitfalls of this approach. Most of them seem to conduct thorough credit checks on clients. And they also offer devices such as 'stop losses' which allow you to set a maximum potential downside before each gamble.

Wheeler says that: 'Our theory is that clients should be able to write out a cheque for £1,000 without undue distress.' This tends to limit the nature of the clientele. 'Our clients are very much male and mostly from the ABC classes, although we do have taxi-drivers and hairdressers.' Although financial expertise is undoubtedly useful for spread betters, Wheeler reckons that only 20 per cent of his clients work in the City.

But the clientele is steadily growing. When IG Index floated on the stock market in 2000, its prospectus revealed that 11,500 clients had bet at least once over the previous twelve months and 20,000 were authorised to bet. In 1998, the group had 5,000 active clients; in 1999, 8,300.

Why, given all the tax advantages, has spread betting not grown more rapidly? Angus McCrone runs a website called Onewaybet.com,[1] which gives news and information on spread betting. 'People have a bit of a mental block with understanding how it (spread betting) works. They have grown up with fixed odds betting. It also has a little bit of an image as a City yuppie thing and as too complicated and high-flying for the ordinary investor,' he says. 'But when people do understand it, it's relatively easy and there are plenty of ways for investors to do it in a conservative way. You can try out some imaginary trades to see how you do. Or you can make some very long-dated bets on the Footsie or on individual shares with the smallest possible stake, so that any losses will be small.'

The industry is certainly undergoing a phase of rapid expansion. Challenging IG Index are City Index, Financial Spreads, SpreadEx (based in Dunstable) and Cantor Index, part of the giant US broker Cantor Fitzgerald.

David Buik, who runs marketing for Cantor, is an old City man, having worked for thirty-five years as a money broker with Exco and Prebon. Initially he didn't think financial spread betting was his cup of tea but he was stimulated by how badly marketed it had been. His younger boss, Lewis Findlay, was previously a bond dealer at Chase Manhattan and J. P. Morgan. Together, they represent the old and new faces of the City. Buik was brought up in the days when a relationship with a client was settled over a good lunch; he is the front man who can charm the clients with a pat on the back and a standing order at the bar. Findlay is the one with the calculating brain who can make sure the odds are calculated correctly and can sniff the mood of the market.

Cantor hopes that it can considerably expand the appeal of spread betting. It runs roadshows round the country in areas of prosperity such as Newcastle, Liverpool, Manchester, Edinburgh and Bristol. Tax, Buik reckons, is the great appeal of the product – there are lots of people in Britain who resent paying it.

But tax is only going to be an issue for the most prosperous part of the population. Investors are already allowed to make more than £7,000 of profits each year from share ownership without paying capital gains tax. On top of that, they can put a fair-sized sum (£7,000 in the 2001–2002 tax year) into an individual savings account – any gains from that are also tax-free.

Buik admits that the growth in the spread betting market was prompted by some special factors. 'The City had shed a lot of people over previous years,' he says. 'One example was foreign exchange dealers made redundant by the launch of the euro.' (The establishment of the euro meant there was no longer a need to trade between European currencies, such as the French franc or the Deutschmark.) 'These were people who had been in the market for a long period of time. They were wealthy and they didn't want to take a job. They had x million in the bank and they thought they'd have some fun with it.'

Another boost came from the demise of floor trading at LIFFE, the London International Financial Futures Exchange. LIFFE was a remarkable institution, where trade was conducted by shouting between dealers in brightly coloured jackets, representing different firms. A smart young man with few qualifications could make a lot of money in a short time on LIFFE, although dealers were often burnt out by thirty.

When competition from Frankfurt in the form of screen-based trading forced LIFFE to abandon the floor-based system, a lot of young risk-takers were left with nowhere to go. According to one or two of the spread betting firms, some are now gambling for a living. 'City traders like the ease of use of spread betting,' says Angus McCrone of Onewaybet, 'and the ability to have leverage.'

Some of these gamblers are taking very short-term positions. Tim Carey, who has been spread betting for eleven years, says his average position is just an hour.[2] 'My style is short, quick profits.' It's really a different version of day trading, which may explain why spread betting had a surge in popularity in 1999. 'The reason the market took off in 1999 was that the day trading mentality arrived from the US,' says Stuart Wheeler.

Debs Harris is a private investor who used to day trade but by late–2000 had switched to spread betting on the Dow and the Footsie. 'It's easier to make money in the current market by shorting [betting on prices to fall],' she says.

Those gamblers who take such short-term bets tend to follow the 'market reversal' strategy – if Footsie has fallen 100 points overnight, they will bet on a rebound in the morning. Stuart Wheeler says that around 80 per cent of clients tend to take the view that a large movement in the market is an over-reaction. This is not a particularly sophisticated level of analysis. Markets can fall for several days in a row – indeed, in September 2000 the FTSE 100 dropped for twelve days out of thirteen. But sophisticated analysis is pretty pointless when you are analysing markets over the short term – such movements tend to be governed by sentiment rather than fundamentals.

Spread betting over the internet represents another opportunity for the industry to expand. Cantor Index launched its service on the website www.cantorindex.com in November 2000. Prices are updated every three seconds on screen and, just as with internet share trading, thousands can be staked with the click of a mouse. Of course, internet clients have to go through the same credit checks as everyone else. And Buik reckons that the majority of Cantor's clients will prefer to deal over the phone, where they can get a 'feel' for the market and negotiate for a slightly better price.

But the internet may attract new clients. 'It will bring in the internet junkies who like to do things online,' says Buik. But another key advantage is anonymity. 'For some people, it is embarrassing to lose money. With the internet, they don't have to lose face by speaking to someone on the phone. And some of our clients fear that, if the dealer knows who they are, he will move the price against them.'

And because internet gamblers don't speak to traders on the phone, the betting companies can offer much lower minimum stakes. That may attract the cautious and those on lower incomes.

There is also scope for expansion at the high-roller end of the market, through contracts for differences or CFDs. These are designed for the 'professional retail punter', says Buik. No stamp duty is charged but capital gains tax is payable on profits. While that sounds like bad news, it isn't in some circumstances.

Say you owned a substantial amount of shares that had already risen in value. You want to protect yourself against a fall in the share price. You can make a down bet or you could sell a CFD. With the former, a rise in the share price would earn you a profit on which you would have to pay tax. But you would be unable to offset your loss on the spread bet against that tax bill. With a CFD, any loss would be tax-deductible, so as a hedge, it is much more tax-efficient.

Within the financial end of the market, the 1999–2000 period was marked by phenomenal growth in betting on individual shares. 'If you are long the FTSE 100 and the market falls, there's nothing you can do,' says Findlay. 'But if you're betting on individual shares, you can hope that some winners will offset the losers.'

Bets on individual shares tend to be made on a long-term basis than bets on the index. Even so, it would be a struggle to describe this as 'investment' rather than speculation. Stuart Wheeler says the average share bet is in place for twenty-three days. That compares with the five years or so that most experts agree is the minimum planning horizon for any equity investor.

But, if you have a gut feeling that a share is going to go up, then a spread bet is probably the best option for maximising your winnings. Sarab Singh, a west London dentist, made £90,000 (tax-free, of course) out of a spread bet on Biocompatibles, a biotechnology group. He trades between appointments using a Reuters pager to keep him up to date with market movements. But he does not allow it to beep, something which is no doubt of great relief to his patients.[3]

According to Stuart Wheeler, gamblers have shown some quite surprising behaviour patterns. 'On indices, clients have been bearish and have tended to short the Dow [the best-known US stock market benchmark],' he says. Perhaps this is not surprising. There has been a body of opinion outside the US that its stock market is too high; professional UK fund managers kept quite a small proportion of their assets in the US during the late 1990s. Being short of the Dow was not a profitable play for much of the late 1990s and Wheeler says clients have not been that good at calling the direction of the overall market. But on individual shares, they have tended to be right more often than not.

Perhaps this success is because clients have followed a different strategy from their approach to the overall market. 'On individual shares,' says Wheeler, 'we expected people would go short, because that's not something they can do elsewhere. In fact, 95 per cent of clients are bullish.'

'Going short' is a term used when people sell a share they don't own in the hope of buying it back at a lower price. That may sound a little screwy. How can you sell something you don't own? It is quite difficult. Normally it requires the investor to borrow shares from someone else who does own them. The owner will lend the shares in return for a fee, equivalent to an interest rate. Essentially, the borrower is gambling that the price will have fallen sufficiently over the period of the loan to offset the financing cost.

The spread betting market sweeps away all these problems. If you think a share price is going to fall, you simply place a down bet. There were plenty of shares in 2000 where this would have been a highly profitable strategy if timed correctly – Lastminute.com, Bookham Technology or Psion, for example. But few people did so.

You can also use down bets to pursue quite sophisticated strategies. Suppose you think that oil giant BP is set to do better than its great rival Shell but you are unsure about the likely direction of the overall market. You could make an up bet on BP and a down bet on Shell. Provided that your original premise was correct, you would make money whatever the fate of the overall market. If BP shares fell 85 per cent but Shell shares dropped 90 per cent, you would still be ahead.

In a way, spread betting means that even the most humble investor can use the same methods as George Soros. 'You can act like your own hedge fund,' says Angus McCrone of Onewaybet, 'going long of this and short of that.'

So how does spread betting fit into the 'easy money' culture? It certainly offers the opportunity for vast gains (and, of course, vast losses) in a short period of time. And, like the Lottery, it is clear to see that the 'wealth' generated is just a transfer – from the losers to the winners.

To be fair to the industry, it does not quite work in the same way as the traditional betting shop, where the old adage is that 'you never see a poor bookmaker'. On a race like the Grand National, bookies will make money if an outsider wins but will lose out if the race is won by a heavily backed favourite. In most cases, the spread-betting firms will hedge the financial bets made by their clients.[4] So if a client bets that the FTSE 100 will rise, the firm will take the same position in the futures market. As long as the spread between the buy and sell prices is greater than the cost of hedging, then the firm will make money.

Unlike a traditional bookmaker, therefore, a spread betting firm can afford to be delighted if its clients make money. If they make money on one bet, after all, they will be more likely to bet again. And the more clients bet, the more money the firms will make.

Lewis Findlay thinks the industry has failed so far to make the most of its advantages. 'There are around 25,000 spread betters out there but already there are 250,000 online share traders. When you consider our tax advantages, that's disappointing. Perhaps it seems too good a deal to people. Perhaps there's still a stigma about betting.'

Online gambling

While spread betting can involve big money, it is at the moment, and is likely to remain, a minority pastime. But the internet has opened up a new, and potentially huge, market for the traditional gambling industry. Market research group Datamonitor reckons the European online betting market could be worth £3.5bn by 2004.

Just like trading on the net (see Chapter 1), gambling on the internet is ridiculously easy. Provided you have mastered the basics of computer use, you can select the winner of the 3.30 at Kempton with one click of a mouse. And the internet has one priceless advantage over staid old betting shops – a net business can be based where it likes. Governments may try to ban betting, or tax it. But they can only tax what they can get hold of. And an internet transaction, conducted down a phone line and using a credit card, can be very hard to tax.

The first person to realise this in the UK was Victor Chandler, a book-maker who specialised in serving high-rolling clients. He started an offshore operation in Gibraltar in 1997, initially over the telephone and then, in 2000, adding a net-based service. At a stroke, his gamblers avoided 6.75 per cent betting duty and a 2.25 per cent racing levy (although Chandler imposed a 3 per cent service charge, which included Gibraltar's 1 per cent betting duty).

The move gave Chandler an instant marketing advantage. Ladbrokes quickly followed suit while Coral bought the Gibraltar-based betting operation Eurobet. Initially, the UK government banned the advertising of such services in the UK. But that proved a pretty flimsy barrier – serious gamblers soon found out about the online opportunity. So in the 2001 Budget, chancellor Gordon Brown came up with a classic British compromise – betting levy of 9 per cent would be scrapped and replaced by a 15 per cent gross tax on the profits of bookmakers. The bookies in turn vowed not to pass the tax on to their clients and to close down their offshore operations. The compromise will not stop gambling on the net, which will retain its advantages of ease and anonymity.

According to Andy Clifton of Ladbrokes, there are considerable differences between the gamblers who use the net and those who use the shops. 'The average stake in a betting shop is £5 but on the internet you can multiply that by a factor of six or seven. Football bets are around 5 per cent of the total in shops but over the internet it is closer to 30 per cent.'

This is good news from the point of view of Ladbrokes. 'One of the great attractions of the internet to us is that we are not cannibalising our business but expanding the market. A lot of people have been put off by the image of betting shops,' says Clifton.

An opportunity which might yet rival the internet for the gambling industry could be digital television. Britons are used to using their TVs – indeed, it is the centrepiece of their living rooms. And, thanks to the remote control, they are already used to 'pointing and clicking' to get services from their TV (the football scores on Ceefax, for example).

Martin Belsham is the man behind Blue Square, the gambling service that is available through Open, the interactive service on Sky Digital, launched in July 2000. Like a good bookmaker, Belsham is hedging his bets about the future for his business. 'We wanted to build a service that was platform-neutral, and had a common back end. Gamblers should see the same service whether they bet through the net, digital TV, broadband or a mobile phone. We are not trying to pre-judge what will be the killer application. We look at ourselves as being in the leisure and entertainment area of the marketplace.'

Blue Square is also linked to BTOpenworld's broadband service (broadband allows for the rapid transmission of more data and images than a conventional phone line). 'We are the only bookmaker on the service,' says Belsham.

Over two years, Blue Square has built up 90,000 customers. The beauty of the digital TV service is that it taps into a different segment of the population, what sociologists call the C2DEs and what the rest of us would call the lower middle classes and the working classes.

In the UK so far, internet usage has tended to be concentrated on the middle classes. It costs a lot to purchase a computer and it still costs a fair amount each month to be connected to the net through the telephone line. For the C2DEs, the internet might only take off if it provided the sole means of watching live football – the 'killer app' that ensured the success of Rupert Murdoch's BSkyB during the 1990s.

Belsham says the digital TV gambling market is quite different from the internet. 'Over the internet, the average bet is around £16–£17, over digital TV it is £5–£6.50.' Digital TV gamblers are also what Belsham describes as 'less sophisticated punters'. They tend to bet on a lot of 'multiples', gambles that require a lot of things to go right to be successful. From time to time, a gambler makes a fortune through some multiple, by predicting, for example, the winners of the Premier League as well as those of Nationwide divisions 1, 2 and 3. The odds against such a prediction are enormous, which is why the payouts are huge but successes are rare.

Smart gamblers usually ignore multiples or each-way bets, in which gains are made (at reduced odds) when a horse comes second, third or (sometimes) fourth. They concentrate on betting heavily on favourites when they are pretty sure they will be successful. The odds may be lower, but winning bets are much more common.

At the moment, Blue Square still faces some of the restrictions that limited TV quizzes in the early days (see Chapter 7). It is illegal to promote or advertise betting on television. But what is promotion? No one stops Channel 4 and BBC1 from showing the odds on a horse race; indeed, Channel 4 makes much play of its 'character' presenter, John McCririck, who uses a bookie's hand signals to illustrate the odds.

When a digital TV customer wants to use the Open service (and bet with Blue Square), the image on the TV has to be entirely replaced with the Blue Square page. (Ideally, from the bookmaker's point of view, the blue square would appear in a corner of the screen while the TV image was still showing.) But the ingenious folks at Blue Square have found a way to get round this. The rival digital service to Sky Digital, OnDigital, has launched its own internet-based service ONnet. Users can accordingly use part of their screen to call up the Blue Square service on ONnet while watching the sporting event of their choice in another corner of the screen. This gets round the Independent Television Commission guidelines since the gambling service is not directly linked to the TV picture; users must make two separate connections. In theory they could be gambling while watching *Songs of Praise*.

But imagine the possibilities that have opened up by combining pictures with real-time gambling information. David Beckham steps up to take a penalty – and in the corner of the screen flashes up the odds that he will score. There are ten fences to go in the Grand National – so the bookie gives odds for whether the leader stays in front. United are 2–0 down at half time but optimists can get 20–1 odds that they will recover to win.

Belsham thinks that digital TV offers some great opportunities. 'The internet market is becoming a lot more crowded, and marketing is quite difficult, whereas with digital TV, you are hotwired into customers.' Digital TV can act as a store window for the business in the family living room with the added advantage that the company knows where its customers live. And like the internet, digital TV gives gamblers a feeling of anonymity – 'You don't have to feel you're making a fool of yourself,' says Belsham.

Wireless access protocol (Wap) phones, which offer internet access, provide yet another way for gambling to enter our lives. The football fan leaves the pub after his pre-match drink and he's in a rush – no chance to get to the bookies. So he simply uses his phone to link to the bookies' website, checks the odds and makes his bet – all while he is still walking into the ground.

As yet, Andy Clifton of Ladbrokes admits, the technology doesn't really live up to the promise. 'Wap is a learning curve for the technology that's coming along. At the moment it'll take you a lot longer to bet via Wap than to ring up and speak to the bookmaker directly.'

But when the third generation of mobile phones comes along using Bluetooth technology (see Chapter 3), data and pictures will be transmitted more clearly and more quickly. 'Hopefully in a year's time you'll be able to have a bet via your mobile and then watch the match on your phone,' says Clifton. That might be a stretch – but a short horse race could be suitable viewing in a mobile phone display.

All these opportunities for gambling might not be possible if the attitude of government and society towards making money quickly had not changed significantly over the last few decades. And it is that to which we will turn in the next chapter.

7

A Cultural Shift

The catalyst for change was the National Lottery. Almost overnight, it changed people's attitudes towards gambling.

Gambling expert

Which county plays cricket at Chester-le-Street? Which King was known as 'the wisest fool in Christendom'? Which king was married to Eleanor of Aquitaine? If you knew the answer to those questions (Durham, James I and Henry II), you could have won £1m on ITV's hit programme *Who Wants to Be a Millionaire?* Of course, you would have needed to answer another fourteen general knowledge questions first. As of April 2001, only one UK competitor had won the jackpot, by answering the third of the above questions. In a neat historical irony, a distant cousin of Camilla Parker-Bowles, the heir to the throne's consort, earned a fortune by knowing the marital details of one of Prince Charles's ancestors.

Thirty years ago, she would not have had the chance to do so. Until quite recently, most Britons were treated like children who needed to be shielded from temptation. There was a strict limit on the prize money that could be paid out on TV quiz shows. Gambling was legal, but made as unappealing as possible. The windows on bookmakers' offices had to be opaque, and the doors closed, so that the impressionable could not look inside.

Ordinary people could still gamble their way to wealth, either through the premium bonds or the pools. The story of Viv Nicholson, the pools winner who vowed to 'Spend, spend, spend', dates back to the early 1960s.

And there were plenty of millionaires, although the tax regime of the time ensured it was harder to get hold of, and enjoy, the wealth.

So it would be foolish to claim that the desire for 'easy money' has not existed in the past. Of course it has. And British culture has not changed beyond all recognition. But there has been a change in the attitude of society and government towards taking risks – just as investors have been encouraged to invest in equities, via PEPs, ISAs and share options, the laws on gambling and TV prize money have been significantly liberalised. It would be unfair to say that the government wants us to gamble like mad (except on the Lottery) but it is certainly not doing much to stop us.

Take the difference between the premium bonds and the National Lottery. Premium bonds were introduced by the Edwardian figure of Harold Macmillan. Bonds could be bought only from the Post Office, rather than any corner newsagent. The prize draw was not shown on national television. And, most crucially of all, to protect citizens from the pernicious vice of gambling, premium bond purchasers can get their money back. In effect, a premium bond is an investment where you gamble your interest, not the capital.

Even though premium bonds seem, in retrospect, a fairly mild form of gambling, they were denounced when first introduced. The Archbishop of Canterbury of the day, Geoffrey Fisher, described the scheme as a squalid enterprise. This disapproval was based on two main precepts. The first was that gambling was immoral – it allowed people to make money in a way that was unrelated to their effort. This objection has been increasingly hard to sustain in recent years. Can one say that the earnings of a rock star or a top football player are really related to their effort? Do they work longer hours than, say, a nurse?

And while investment bankers may work extremely hard in return for their enormous salaries, are their rewards really justified? As far as society is concerned, is the work of an investment banker particularly useful when compared with that of a teacher or doctor?

Clearly, the answer is no. But society has decided that the earnings of such people should not be restricted. This is in part for sound practical reasons; unless there was a worldwide cap on earnings, a restriction in one country would simply prompt talented individuals to move elsewhere.

There is also a theoretical justification. The argument for limiting earnings is that there is a set 'pot' of wealth that has to be shared. Wealth had to be redistributed by punitive taxation to stop some people from getting more than their fair share. But this view is out of fashion: the theory is that talented people, if properly rewarded, create wealth and jobs for the rest of us.

The same principle applies to the money that can be earned from investing in shares. From the left-wing point of view, this is 'unearned' and should be heavily taxed. But the free market argument is that it is necessary for people to save if industry is to have the money it needs to invest. Even traders, by providing liquidity to the share market, are performing a useful function; without liquidity fewer people would be willing to invest in the first place, for fear they would be unable to get back their money when they needed it.

Which side of this argument you favour probably depends on your politics. But the free market argument now seems to be held by the majority. In such circumstances, anything goes. It was lucky for David Beckham that he was born with the ability to kick a ball better than most. He has earned millions as a consequence because, in a free market, Manchester United is willing to pay for his ability.

Until the early 1960s, fame would have been his only reward; until then, players' wages were subject to a maximum limit. Cricket was dominated by amateurs; rugby union was exclusively played by them. But now sport is perceived as a potential road to riches by many working-class people.

And if you can make a million by kicking a ball, why not grant millions to people who are lucky enough to pick the six winning numbers in the Lottery?

The more fundamental argument against gambling is that it is a mug's game and the mugs tend to come from the poorest classes. The people should be protected from their worst instincts. The principle is no different from banning the use of hard drugs or from restricting the hours when alcohol can be purchased. Without the nanny state to protect them, the people will sink into the mire.

These objections were raised when the National Lottery was introduced in 1994. The Methodist church protested that it would 'induce poor people to spend money that they cannot afford on prizes that they are unlikely to win'. Some on the left denounced the Lottery as a 'prole tax' – a levy likely to fall disproportionately on the less well-off. Indeed, the Social Trends Survey 2000 did find that skilled manual labourers were the most regular Lottery players, with professionals the least regular.

The current National Lottery is not Britain's first. According to James

Raven, director of studies in history, Magdalene College, Cambridge,[1] lottery money built Westminster Bridge and established the British Museum. Lotteries were a standard fund-raiser for cash-strapped governments in the eighteenth century.

But lotteries fell into disrepute after tickets started to be bought by the poor rather than just the wealthy. Raven reports that a select committee of 1808 concluded that because of lotteries 'idleness, dissipation and poverty are increased, domestic comfort is destroyed, madness often created; crimes, subjecting the perpetrators of them to the punishment of death, are committed and even suicide itself is produced'.

Lotteries did not last long after that. The idea did not really fit in with Victorian morality at all: neither with the evangelical desire to protect the poor from vice nor with the Samuel Smiles view that the way out of the gutter was through hard work.

By the 1960s and 1970s, making money quickly seemed to be beyond the reach of most people. The vast majority did not own shares, not even in the companies they worked for (indeed, a lot of people worked for nationalised industries). Thirty years ago, the class structure seemed more rigid. Working-class children could expect to follow their fathers down the mine or into the shipyard or to the car plant. Middle-class children would go into the professions. Schools did little to discourage children from following the same rigid career path.

Wage differentials were much narrower than they are now. Union power enhanced the wages of certain 'blue collar' professions like railwaymen and printers. And, in part because of union power, a job as a manager in a corporation held little appeal to many middle-class graduates; a lot of hassle for a pretty meagre reward.

There was little incentive to set up a business on your own. Extra income was heavily taxed. Banks were cautious about lending money to new businesses and there was no such thing as venture capital.

Ostentatious wealth was frowned upon. It was an egalitarian rather than a religious matter. The old story about the American and British workers had more than a ring of truth to it. The British worker sees the boss's Rolls-Royce and thinks: 'Why should he be allowed to have a car like that?' The US worker says: 'How can I get one?'

Michael Douglas had yet to proclaim that 'Greed was good' and the moral guardians of the nation would not have agreed with him in any case. TV quiz shows were a particular worry. The Broadcasting Act placed a duty on the Independent Television Authority to limit the value of prizes awarded. Even so, the Pilkington Committee of 1960 detected 'an erosion of moral standards in the spectacle of valuable prizes too easily won'.

According to the official history of independent television,[2] 'The maximum permissible monetary value of prizes was fixed and raised, with reluctance, only in step with inflation.' The maximum was £1,000 until 1975 – although subject to a classic British compromise, which allowed the maximum to be an average over four programmes, so that *Sale of the Century* could offer a car as top prize. By 1981, the top prize had become £3,250, subject to a weekly average of £1,750.

But such luxury should not be easily won. According to the official history: 'the need to have some recognisable and defensible relationship between the value of the reward and the skill and effort called for from contestants was firmly emphasised'. The most popular quiz show of the 1980s, *Mastermind*, combined tough questions on arcane subjects with the token prize of an engraved glass bowl.

'The original ITV legislation was written from a Methodist/puritan and rather nannyish standpoint,' says Chris Dunkley, TV critic of the *Financial Times*. 'They took the view that people should not be greedy. In the US, you had the $64,000 question but in the UK, you couldn't win anything remotely like that. The prizes on *Double Your Money* or *Take Your Pick* were pretty laughable. The goods on the conveyor belt on *The Generation Game* were worth about the price of a BR ticket.'

There were some similarities in style between the old and the new formats. A book called *The Mirror in the Corner* by Peter Black describes how *Double Your Money* was a forerunner of *Who Wants to Be a Millionaire?*[3] 'The first questions were picked to settle the contestants' nerves and earn some quick laughs, e.g. "Is a man who looks down rabbit holes a borough surveyor?"' But these questions earned the winner £1, £2, £4 and so on, rather than the £100, £200, £300 of the modern show.

As the prizes grew larger, the programme makers ratcheted up the tension. Contestants on *Double Your Money* sat in a soundproof glass box while a clock ticked away – note how in *Who Wants?*, the background sound (designed to mimic a heartbeat) gets louder as the competition progresses.

And despite the poor prizes, quiz shows were astonishingly popular. The official history describes how the Independent Television Authority was forced to remind some companies that they could not run more than two rewards shows a week in their peak-time schedule. In 1973, the weekly per-mitted maximum became two network shows in peak time, one net-worked afternoon show and one local show. In the course of 1980, more than twenty different reward shows were networked.

The history comments that 'serious-minded critics did not desist from castigating them as public celebrations of sinful greed, but they provided half an hour or more of escapism at home for millions, a memorable evening out for hundreds as studio audiences, and the event of a lifetime for a happy few'.

One not-so-serious minded critic was Clive James who wrote in the *Observer* that: 'There is a limit to the sense in which it is true to say that peo-ple should be given what they want. The limit can be set at the point where the spectacle on offer ceases to be human. There is something inhuman about training quiz show contestants to jump up and down with excite-ment, faint with surprise and yell lines of special material even more fatu-ous than the host is reading off his cue cards.'[4]

By the late 1980s, quiz shows had rather gone out of fashion. Controls on prizes were lifted by the Broadcasting Act of 1990, but it was eight years be-fore the production company Celador seized the opportunity and launched *Who Wants to Be a Millionaire?* 'When *Who Wants to Be a Millionaire?* was created, nobody thought it would work,' recalls Chris Dunkley.

But the show was an instant success, topping the ratings and repeating the trick when transplanted to the US. As if to prove there are still some cultural differences between the US and the UK, America created its first millionaire before the British original had done so. Perhaps that reflected the American willingness to 'go for it' compared with British caution. (Certainly the first US millionaire was distinctly cocky. He used his 'phone a friend' option on the $1m question to call his father. 'Dad,' he said, 'I've just called to tell you I'm a millionaire. I know the answer to this question.' The average Briton would want to slap him across the face.)

There is an interesting contrast between the approach of the UK TV contestants and their counterparts in the stock market. The contestants are keen to hang on to their winnings – they will stop at £64,000 or £16,000 rather than risk losing money in the search for a million. Private investors have the urge to stay in the game; people like John Delaney (see Chapter 1) might take some money out of the market but will not stop trading even if they reach £1m.

Perhaps this is because the dilemma is much clearer in the game show format. A wrong answer in *Who Wants to Be a Millionaire?* could lose as much as £468,000 and there is only ever one right answer. The contestants have a pretty good idea whether they are guessing or whether they genuinely know the answer. In the stock market, however, you are always guessing. There is an almost infinite variety of right and wrong answers. And there is no one point at which an investor is asked the £1m question – the process is much more gradual. The stock market encourages contestants to stay in the game.

Gambling

The official attitude to gambling has gone through the same change that has liberalised TV game shows. For a long time, there was a definite feeling that the nation needed to be protected from its gambling instinct. Dr Gerda Reith, a lecturer in sociology at Glasgow University and an expert on gambling, explains: 'The Gaming Act was very paternalistic. You had to join a casino in person two days before you wanted to gamble. Casinos and bingo halls couldn't be in the phone book.'

The fact that bets are not enforceable in law dates back to the Gaming Act of 1845. According to a report by KPMG, the rule was established to 're-move the state's involvement from the business of settling gambling debts. The court system had begun to get clogged with outstanding cases' but also because of the belief that 'those foolish enough to gamble should suffer the consequences and not expect the state to help them'.[5]

A parliamentary commission on gambling in 1978 said the government had a 'duty positively to protect people from over-indulging. Local authorities should have the opportunity of preventing housewives from being deflected into prize bingo establishments during their morning shopping in the high street.'

The authorities had perfectly good social reasons for their attitude. Gambling certainly can be addictive and it is easy for the poor to lose a very large proportion of their disposable income in the betting shop. (It isn't just a problem for the poor; many an aristocratic family has been ruined by a dissolute heir's bad luck with cards.)

In the US, a strong puritanical streak meant that gambling was also tightly controlled. Interstate gambling was banned. The 'numbers racket' that was occasionally referred to in Hollywood films about the Mafia was essentially no more than a lottery.

For around a century, the only places where Americans could legally gamble were Las Vegas, in the Nevada desert, and Atlantic City on the New Jersey shore. But the US, like the UK, has been through a gambling transformation. First, a number of states started to use lotteries as fund-raising devices. Secondly, native Americans exploited their rights to run casinos on their reservations. Then, some states, such as Mississippi, agreed to allow gambling on riverboats as a means of rejuvenating run-down areas (and it is hard to get a more run-down area than some of the poorer parts of Mississippi). Soon even conservative and religious states were liberalising their laws, for fear their citizens would simply gamble in other states, and take vital tax revenue with them.

Anyone who has been to Las Vegas or Atlantic City will know that the place is a cathedral of gambling. Even when you sit at the bar to have a drink, you are confronted with a video poker machine designed to gobble up your change. Hotel rooms are deliberately kept cheap to attract as many guests as possible.

Vegas may be tacky, but any student of human nature will find it worth a visit. Most fascinating of all are the vast hangar-like rooms filled with slot machines and with (often elderly) tourists methodically inserting coins from plastic buckets. Any visiting alien would logically assume that these machines were deities that humans were attempting to placate, or that they were some kind of queen bee that the human drones were conditioned to feed. Certainly, the players often look hypnotised; their eyes rarely leave the screen.

The rooms are open twenty-four hours a day; in the artificial light, it is impossible to tell whether it is morning or night. And the sound of a million levers being pulled and counters whirring is almost deafening, as if one had wandered into a factory in the early days of mass production.

The palaces of Las Vegas appeal to some core element in human nature. 'Gambling is ancient and ubiquitous, you find it in every culture and it is almost always condemned,' says Dr Reith. GamCare, a charity that helps people with gambling problems, estimates that around 72 per cent of the UK population gambles. A survey found that over half the population had gambled in the week before the interview.

And it is this gambling instinct that the UK government tapped when it introduced the National Lottery. Gamblers were given an excuse to indulge their vice, in that a proportion of their stake would go to a motley group of good causes – sport, the arts, millennium-related activities and a few charities.

'The catalyst for change was the National Lottery. Almost overnight, it changed people's attitudes towards gambling. It popularised and legitimised gambling and opened the way for the ever-increasing accessibility of gambling activities,' said Paul Bellringer, a director of GamCare.

'If it wasn't for the Lottery you would still have the Puritans saying "It's OK to bet once a year but if I bet any more I'll start to be an alcoholic and divorce my wife,"' says Martin Belsham of the betting group Blue Square.

Dr Reith agrees: 'The idea of getting rich quick has always been around. But there has definitely been a climate change. The introduction of the National Lottery has brought out the urge in the population and made it visible.' GamCare's survey found that 65 per cent of the population had bought a Lottery ticket over the previous year while only 13 per cent had made a bet on a horse race over the same period.

Once the government had given the green light to gambling for its own benefit, it found it harder to resist liberalisation elsewhere. The rest of the gaming industry started to moan about unfair competition. The Home Office continued the gradual relaxation of the stringent restrictions on betting shops, imposed by the Betting, Gaming and Lotteries Act of 1963.

In 1986 (admittedly well before the Lottery), TV pictures were first allowed in betting shops and light refreshments could be served. In 1993, shops were allowed to open in the evening. In 1995, shops were allowed to open on Sundays, windows could show advertising displays and customers could be served 'hand-held snacks'. (What a wonderfully British rule. How many innocents would be lured into a life of vice by a sausage roll?) In 1996, shops were allowed to offer slot machines with a prize of no more than £10. In December 1999, home secretary Jack Straw announced a comprehensive review of the industry and the creation of an independent review body to design a new regulatory structure. At the time of writing, the review was not complete. But it was widely expected that there would be fundamental reform, with a single regulatory body established to oversee the entire gambling industry. That would mean that the rules and regulations covering the various types of gambling would be made consistent.

The gambling industry is now a significant part of British life. According to consultants KPMG, Britons make bets to the tune of more than £42bn a year and the industry employs over 170,000 people, directly and indirectly.

Gambling is now ever-present in the coverage of sporting events on television, when it used to be limited to horse racing. Spread betting, which allows for gambling on a host of sporting details, has leapt into the national consciousness. 'During the rugby World Cup of 1999, I noticed that all the newspapers were talking about spread bets,' says GamCare's Paul Bellringer. 'Spread betting has certainly caused some people to beat a path to our counselling service.' Spread betters made up around 8 per cent of GamCare callers in 1999.

As yet, gambling liberalisation has not led to significant social problems. 'Most people manage to keep it under control,' says Paul Bellringer. 'We think that problem gamblers amount to around 0.8 per cent, so that works out at around 400,000 people. Still, that is more than the numbers of heroin or cocaine addicts.'

But Bellringer thinks that the new opportunities for gambling outlined in Chapter 6 could increase the number of addicts. 'We are worried about the growing use of new technologies such as the internet and interactive television. There have to be safeguards put into place. Staff involved should be trained in recognising warning signs. There should be pauses built into the play to give people time to reflect, because gambling can be so totally absorbing. Like alcohol, gambling can be a poor master but a good servant.'

Both GamCare and Gamblers Anonymous have spotted a new breed of addict in recent years – people hooked on stock market trading. As we saw in Chapter 1, the approach taken by many investors to share trading is pretty hard to distinguish from gambling. There ought to be a difference, of course. 'With investment, you expect to make a gain. With gambling, you expect to make a loss,' says Bellringer. But frequent trading is more like speculation than genuine investment.

Professor Shiller of Yale says that gambling was also immensely popular in the 1920s, another boom time for the stock markets, when the criminal gangs in the US that exploited the prohibition of alcohol 'diversified' into lottery and roulette-style games.[6]

'A spillover from gambling to financial volatility may come about because gambling, and the institutions that promote it, yield an inflated estimate of one's own ultimate potential for good luck, a heightened interest in how one performs compared with others and a new way to stimulate oneself out of a feeling of boredom or monotony.'

He adds that gambling 'suppresses natural inhibitions against taking risks and some of the gambling contracts, in particular the lotteries, superficially resemble financial markets'. Indeed, investors in stocks may be no more scientific than gamblers on horse races, making their selections on the basis of the name alone, or on a tip in a newspaper. The very existence of day trading, and the short timespan typical of spread betters, shows that many investors do not bother with fundamental analysis, which cannot possibly predict daily movements.

Finance and the media

It may be a coincidence, but the liberalisation of gambling laws has been accompanied by a greater public level of interest in finance. That in turn has been reflected in a greater level of coverage in the media. Twenty years ago, the only mainstream broadcast coverage of business was *The Money Programme* on BBC2 and *Moneybox* and *The Financial World Tonight* on Radio 4.

The newspapers all had their business sections, of course, but the main focus was on the activities of the tycoons of their day – City editors would saunter back from lunch at the Savoy with Lord Hanson to pass on a few nuggets of his wisdom. Apart from the *Daily Mail*'s Money Mail, personal finance topics were given little coverage and were regarded as a journalistic backwater.

All that has changed for one good reason – advertising revenue. The arrival of personal equity plans in the 1980s created a new market. From the marketing point of view, it helped that PEPs were based on the tax year. That means you had an instant annual deadline and a compelling slogan – buy now before April 5. And it helped the media that the PEP rules were fairly complicated and the choice of plans was overwhelming. Financial services groups were desperate to differentiate their PEP from those offered by other companies. PEPs have been replaced by ISAs but the advertising binge has continued. Few newspapers will be without their ISA supplement when March comes around.

There is much greater interest in the City in the mid-market and tabloid papers than there used to be – as the mere fact that the *Mirror* bothered with a City Slickers column showed. A survey in the *Evening Standard* found that the *Daily Mail* and *Daily Express* between them ran twice as many City stories in 2000 as they did in 1970.[7]

Television has also become aware of the potential of finance. The people who watch financial programmes tend to be well-off and to attract advertisers. The Money Channel started broadcasting in February 2000 on

BSkyB's digital TV service. It was the brainchild of Adam Faith, the former pop singer, and Paul Killik, head of the eponymous stockbroking firm. The company's offices are sited in an industrial estate near the Shadwell tube station in east London. As an occasional guest on the channel, I find it a weird juxtaposition; you leave the station to trek through run-down council estates and past a queue of pensioners waiting for the Post Office to open; ten minutes later, you are sitting in a hi-tech, modernist studio, discussing billion-pound takeover deals.

Tony Hobman, the Money Channel's chief executive, says the existence of the channel has only become possible in the last few years. 'People are more interested in money. At one level, it's vaguely sexy – there is ever-greater sophistication of presentation. And people perceive the state as no longer providing the traditional backstops so they have to provide for themselves.'

But the key step, he feels, is the creation of digital TV, which has allowed the creation of specialist channels and the potential for interactivity. Specialist channels don't need to be ratings grabbers. 'People will watch specialist channels when they have a need for them, rather than watch all day,' says Hobman. He claims that 130,000 people watch the channel each week for more than three minutes. While that's tiny by the standards of *Coronation Street*, the key for financial advertisers is that these are the right kind of people. 'We have the highest proportion of ABC1 viewers of any channel.'

The internet also creates an exciting business opportunity. 'If you can generate powerful compelling content, you can make it available through the internet as well as the TV. We have generic advice in the archive on things like pensions and mortgages that clearly has value.'

In its early months, the bulk of the Money Channel's revenue came from the traditional vehicle of advertising. But Hobman thinks that digital TV's interactivity gives the company a potentially lucrative opportunity. 'The financial industry is relatively inefficient in generating leads, and they will spend £70–£100 to get one. We can charge a third of that to get them people who show interest via interactive service.'

The idea is quite simple. An advert for, say, Standard Life will appear on the screen. Viewers wishing to receive more information will be able to press a button on their remote control. In theory, since the system already has the viewer's name and address, the brochure can then be sent straight to them. The Money Channel gets a payment; the insurance company sends a brochure to someone who's genuinely interested (as opposed to someone who'll just throw it in a bin); the viewer gets the brochure he or she requested. Everyone's happy.

At a later stage, viewers may be able to conduct transactions in the same way. The advert might be for a Japanese unit trust. Viewers tantalised by the temptations of Tokyo will be able to fill in an application form on screen, enter their bank details and send the money right off. For that to happen, however, the channel will have to overcome some big regulatory hurdles – has the viewer received the right advice, have they been given sufficient information, and so on. That may not be the channels' only problem. The big fall in the stock market in late 2000 and 2001 cut investor enthusiasm for the stock market. Shares in the Money Channel slipped to just a few pence as the market worried about the group's long-term survival.

The new share trading culture also opened opportunities in the more traditional media. *Shares* magazine couldn't have timed it better; it was first published in September 1999, a month or so before the take-off in trading volumes. Editor Ross Greenwood had been in charge of Australia's largest business and personal finance magazines and set up an Aussie version of *Shares*. He was invited to London to do the same for the MSM publishing group.

'We didn't aim to be a general personal finance magazine, nor a business magazine pitched at the City. We just wanted to focus on shares,' he says. The magazine takes a light and bright approach to investing – lots of pictures and graphics and short, snappy articles. The 2 November 2000 issue had a picture of Oasis on the cover[8] and snaps of Madonna, Posh'n'Becks and Liz Hurley inside.

'When you've got very low interest rates, there is more interest in the high risk and high return share market,' says Greenwood. 'People have begun to think: am I as smart as the professionals? Is investing really so difficult? They'd been given more information than ever before by the internet. People felt the gaps in their knowledge were being filled very rapidly.'

Although there is lots of information available over the net for free, Greenwood has found that 27,000 people are willing to shell out £2.30 a week for his magazine. 'Our belief is that long term, for whatever reason, people will still pay for a paper product. The internet is more like radio, people expect it to be free and pay for itself.'

Interestingly, Greenwood has noticed that the magazine's newsstand sales are linked to the volume of trading rather than the overall level of the market. When people are trading heavily, they buy the magazine – perhaps for ideas on which shares to buy. He worries sometimes that the sensible approach taken by his magazine is not always appreciated. During the heady days of late 1999 and early 2000, suggesting that technology shares were overvalued was not a popular stance. 'The public's imagination was captured by the hi-tech boom,' he recalls. 'Many investors didn't want to hear the bad news and some novices got into the market on a promise. Their ideal story would be "Five shares that can double in three months".'

So will general interest in the stock market survive a protracted bear market? Many in the media certainly hope so. 'The Money Channel was not set up as a service for day traders,' says Tony Hobman. 'Whether the market is going up or down, it should still be interesting for investors.' 'The readers may just want share tips but we've got to believe in education over the long term,' says Greenwood. 'If they lose all their money, they won't stay subscribers.'

If they can survive the downturn in the market demographics may be a powerful factor in favour of the Money Channel and *Shares* magazine. There is a general feeling that the 'baby boomers', those people born in the 1945–70 era, will have to become more interested in the stock market if they want to be well provided for in their old age. The government will be of little help. And that brings us to one of the most powerful drivers of cultural change in the last twenty-five years – the Conservative government of 1979–97.

That government unleashed a whole raft of changes that directly led to today's more money-conscious climate. In no particular order, these were:

Change in the pension rules. One of the earliest acts of the government was to break the link between state pensions and average earnings. The pension was instead up-rated each year in line with consumer prices. Since earnings rise faster than prices, the effect was to save the government a lot of money, and to steadily reduce the relative value of the pension.

Many people now realise that they cannot rely on the state to deliver a very prosperous old age. So they have to provide for themselves. And, given that equities deliver the best long-term returns, that has forced a greater focus on the stock market. Personal pensions, although dogged by allegations of mis-selling, have become widespread, particularly among the self-employed or mobile workers who do not fit neatly into traditional pension schemes. The Labour government is trying to encourage greater saving among the lower paid by introducing stakeholder pensions, which are designed to be flexible and have lower charges.

Top rate tax reduction. The top rate of tax on earned income was 83 per cent. Even as late as 1988, it was 60 per cent. By cutting the top rate of tax to 40 per cent, the Conservatives dramatically improved the take-home pay of top earners. And by reducing the attractiveness of perks like company cars, they shifted the emphasis of executive pay from status symbols to hard cash.

Privatisation. Moving industries like telecoms, power and water into private hands meant that vast parts of the economy started to be run on a profit-seeking basis. The privatisations also put shares in the hands of millions of investors who would otherwise never have gone near the market. And it also taught them that shares tend to go up. The government's aim was to create 'popular capitalism' and it was pretty successful.

Labour reform. The Conservatives were determined to reduce the power of the unions. They achieved this by restricting picketing, imposing ballots on strike action and union membership and (perhaps most importantly of all) by facing down the miners' strike of 1984.

The lasting effects were manifold. First, it allowed the wholesale restructuring of British industry. Much misery was caused but resources were released from old unprofitable areas of the economy so they could be put to use elsewhere. Secondly, managers were able to run their companies on a more flexible and profitable basis. Thirdly, workers of all types lost security. Workers in manufacturing lost out in the recession of the early 1980s; in the recession of the early 1990s, it was the turn of white-collar workers. No longer can you start a job after school or university and expect to stay with the same employer until retirement.

This change may in itself, believes Dr Reith, have helped to encourage the growth of gambling. 'The idea of a job for life has been eroded,' she says. 'There is a climate of insecurity and nothing can be taken for granted. That encourages gambling. If you can't work for wealth yourself, it's tempting to gamble.'

Liberalisation of the financial markets. It is hard to imagine now but, up until 1979, Britons' ability to buy foreign currency was severely restricted. There were even limitations on the amount of money you could take on holiday. The abolition of those controls not only gave a tremendous boost to activity in the City – a home of 'easy money' if ever there was one – it was also the first step in the globalisation of the UK economy. As the economy has become more global, UK firms have merged with those overseas competitors – and imported some of their customs. In particular, chief executives have been able to draw salary comparisons with their much richer counterparts in the US.

Also, by freeing banks from restrictions, it became much easier for individual consumers to get credit. In bygone times, one actually had to go cap in hand to the building society to ask for a loan to buy a house – now they compete to offer you money. Credit card use has exploded. By early 2001, consumer debt as a proportion of household income had reached record levels.

Liberal tax treatment of share options. As outlined in Chapter 5, share options were designed to bring the interests of managers in line with those of shareholders. Whether or not they have done that, they have certainly created the opportunity for many executives (and some employees) to get rich.

PEPs and ISAs. The government actively encouraged the growth of share ownerships by the use of tax-free savings schemes. PEPs (personal equity plans) were first introduced in 1987 by the then chancellor Nigel Lawson. Gains from shares held within a PEP were free of income and capital gains tax.

In what turned out to be a recurring theme, the initial growth of PEPs was hampered by some stupid and petty rules. A maximum of £2,400 could be invested in any year in a PEP at first. That sum was not big enough to interest many financial services providers, nor was it big enough to give PEP buyers a properly diversified portfolio. The obvious answer was to let investors put unit trusts into a PEP. (Unit trusts are collective savings vehicles specifically designed to give small investors the chance to own a broad spread of the market.) Lawson, however, in an attempt to encourage direct equity ownership, limited unit trust PEPs to £900 a year. The PEP industry did not take off until the rules on unit trusts were relaxed.

PEPs were highly successful, but in a limited way. Lots of middle-class people used them to build up large portfolios of shares on which they paid no tax. In effect, the general taxpayer was subsidising the better-off.[9]

So when the Labour government was elected in 1997, it decided, in its wisdom, to come up with its own tax-efficient scheme, the ISA or individual savings account. This was designed to encourage a wider group of people to save. But it was even more complicated than PEP. Investors can have either a maxi-ISA or three separate mini-ISAs, one based on equities, one on cash deposits and one on insurance. Money did flow into the cash and shares ISAs but the insurance element was a flop.

Nevertheless, the amount of money invested in these schemes is substantial. The value of unit trust PEPs grew from £3.3bn in 1992 to £60.4bn in 1999, or £67.2bn if ISAs are included. Nearly £11bn worth of PEPs were sold in 1998 alone.

Sadly, investors have shown a degree of irrationality in their approach to PEP and ISA investment. The sensible approach would be to spread the annual investment over the tax year so that the investor does not put in all of his or her money at a peak in the market. Instead, there tends to be a mad rush at the end of the tax year. In the last few months before PEPs were abolished in the spring of 1999, nearly £5bn of PEPs were sold. ISA sales were buoyant in March 2000 when the Techmark index was 5,700 and the FTSE 100 index was 6,600. A year later, when the Techmark was under 2,000 and the Footsie was around 5,500, sales slumped. It is a strange business when a cut in prices caused a slump in sales; if consumers behaved like stock market investors, Harrod's would be empty in January.

Property market boom. Whether the Thatcher government was responsible for this is a moot point, but it undoubtedly happened on its watch. By liberalising financial markets and by encouraging the sale of council houses to tenants, Thatcher certainly gave the property boom a helping hand.

By the end of the 1980s, there was hardly a dinner party in the land that did not discuss the soaring price of the participants' houses. Some people may have made a greater paper profit from their house each year than they earned in their jobs. This was the ultimate 'easy money' in that all you had to do was live in the place and you were guaranteed to make a profit.

The golden rule was 'borrow as much as you can to buy the biggest house you can afford'. This rule was the result of inflation, which rewards borrowers and penalises savers. Inflation eroded the real value of the mortgage debt, which was fixed. At the same time, inflation increased salaries, making it progressively easier to afford the interest payments on the debt.

There are some similarities between the late-1990s enthusiasm for shares and the late-1980s property boom. In both cases, investors ceased to worry about whether valuations made sense – whether a semi-detached in Neasden was really worth half a million. All that mattered was that someone else would be willing to pay a higher price in six months' or a year's time.

The property boom collapsed as all debt-financed booms are bound to do. A final spree was unleashed in 1988 when then chancellor Nigel Lawson announced the phasing out of 'double tax relief' – when two people buying a house together could each get tax relief on the first £30,000 of debt. But interest rates were slowly being forced up to combat inflation – a problem caused in part by the housing market. Homeowners were spending part of their house profits, a phenomenon known as equity withdrawal.

Once it became difficult for people to afford mortgage payments, they became forced sellers of their properties. Rising prices for any asset depend on demand exceeding supply. But at some point in the late 1980s, the balance tipped – supply started to exceed demand. Prices started to fall. That destroyed the argument for buying houses as an investment and further cut demand. In turn, lower demand meant lower prices and so on. High interest rates also prompted a recession, causing many people to lose their jobs. Some people had their houses repossessed; others were trapped in 'negative equity' where the value of their debt was greater than the value of the house.

The collapse of the property market may have made people in the 1990s more cautious about borrowing too much to buy a house. But one can plausibly argue that it did foster the cult of speculation – by teaching Britons it was possible to earn a large amount of money in a short period of time, with little effort.

Many of the above changes were positive. As someone who grew up in the 1970s, amidst all the strikes, inflation and chaos, it is pretty easy to see that the UK is a lot better place now than it was back then. But it has also changed in less appealing ways. The gap between rich and poor is both wider and more glaring – I cannot recall ever seeing someone begging on the streets when I was a teenager but now the sight is commonplace.

The rich have always been with us. And the trend for them to display their riches – conspicuous consumption – waxes and wanes. There was a waxing in the 1980s, the era of *Dallas* and *Dynasty*, of shoulder pads, designer labels, Porsches and 'greed is good'. And it waxed again in the mid 1990s, an era of cigar bars, shopaholics and *Hello!* magazine, which allowed the plebs to have a glimpse of the lives of the rich and famous. Gossip columnists wrote breathlessly of the 'It girls', glamorous socialites who never turned right when entering an aeroplane.

Of course, these trends are never uniform. The really new money, the dotcom riches, seemed more inclined to hide their riches, hanging around in coffee bars, wearing shorts and sneakers. But it may be merely a matter of time before they start to show off their wealth; Microsoft founder Bill Gates, for example, has constructed a hi-tech Xanadu of a house outside Seattle. But then his fortune was founded way back in the 1980s.

Unsurprisingly, conspicuous consumption is most obvious (and most tolerated by the rest of the population) in boom times like the 1920s or 1980s. The rich did not flaunt their wealth during the 1940s (wartime, austerity and rationing) or the 1970s (recession, strikes and high taxation.)

But even amidst economic prosperity, the recent extremes of wealth seem to have created a backlash. The Stop the City marches of 1999 and the riots at the World Trade Organisation meeting in Seattle in 2000 indicate that there is a significant minority of people who dislike the modern materialist culture. Their views may not always be coherent – covering everything from environmentalism to workers' rights – but their passion is unmistakable. A recession in the West might swing the political pendulum their way.

Conclusion

A change has occurred in British culture over the last twenty years. Money-making may once have been seen as the unspeakable in pursuit of the unattainable, to misquote Oscar Wilde, but it has ceased to be so.

The pursuit of money for its own end used to be seen as a rather sordid activity. Under the old class system, the aristocracy, who already had money, looked down on the middle classes who indulged in 'trade'. And the middle classes wanted nothing more than to aspire to the status and habits of the aristos. In literature, financiers like Merdle[1] in Dickens' *Little Dorrit* or Melmotte in Trollope's *The Way We Live Now* were portrayed as unscrupulous scoundrels, destined to bring ruin on themselves and all who believed in them.

Religion has always had an ambivalent attitude towards money-making. The money-grubbing tactics of the medieval Catholic church was one of the factors that prompted the Reformation. Usury, the earning of interest from money, was once condemned. Since merchants and governments always have a need to borrow money, the task often fell to Jews to be the lenders; and with breathtaking hypocrisy, Christians took their money and despised them for providing it. Since any church has to make its peace with the secular authorities, neither Catholic nor Protestant church has placed much emphasis on the biblical injunction that a rich man should 'sell all you have and give to the poor' in order to get into heaven.

In one famous historian's view,[2] the tenets of the Protestant religion were responsible for the growth of capitalism. But whether or not that thesis was correct, in Protestant eyes there was a clear distinction between the virtues of thrift, hard work and the ability to build a business on the one hand – and outright speculation on the other.

It is interesting that the modern urge to make millions is so strong at a time when the influence of organised religion in the UK has faded. In a way you could see the Lottery (and *Who Wants to Be a Millionaire?*) as a substitute for religion.

Marx said that religion was the 'opiate of the masses'. By promising the poor a blissful life in heaven (provided they bowed the knee to the established social order), the ruling classes encouraged them to accept their dreadful lives on earth.

Sitting on a cloud playing the harp is all very well, but to the modern man or woman a more tangible form of heaven would be sitting on a Caribbean island, drinking a Margarita. Working life may be full of stress. But if we keep buying the Lottery tickets and ringing the TV contestant line, maybe, just maybe, we'll get to our earthly version of Paradise.

And, just as religion has faded, so has the egalitarian/socialist philosophy. The fall of communism and the long electoral rule of the Conservative Party has caused a shift in UK politics – the modern Labour Party's policies are more akin to those of the old Tory 'wets'. We hear nothing about 'soaking the rich' these days. Extremes of wealth are perceived as a 'price worth paying' for economic progress.

The UK economy does look a lot healthier than it did twenty years ago when labour relations were poor and governments were subsidising smokestack industries that were uncompetitive in global terms. The easy money culture must have played its part in that.

We need people to take risks to make progress. We have to allow some people to get millions by setting up new businesses – if we do not, other countries will attract such people and dominate new industries and all of us will be the poorer.

But as I have argued throughout the book, for most people the hope of overnight riches is going to be an illusion. We are not going to become millionaires through the Lottery, or gambling, or on a TV quiz show. Nor are the vast majority of us going to make millions through the stock market or through share options. Indeed, the same gambling mentality that embraces the Lottery reduces investors' chances of success, by increasing trading costs and encouraging irrational investment strategies.

Society is also coarser as a result of the cultural change. Greed used to be seen as shameful rather than something to be celebrated in a game show format. Britons used to be reticent in discussing money, for fear of seeming boastful or insensitive.

Financial news has come out of the ghetto – but when the media popularise a subject, they have a tendency to over-simplify. From the investor's point of view, the right format for *Show Me the Money* would be a two- or three-hour programme every year in which both the investment criteria of the participants and the financial details of the companies involved would be discussed in full. But that would not make good television. As it is, the half-hour weekly format does not encourage good investment tactics.

So will the cultural change last? Having criticised the forecasting record of others in the course of this book, it is time to stick my neck out and make some predictions of my own. But, sadly, there are no share tips.

Trading

The internet will gradually replace the telephone as the primary means of trading shares. It is cheap, quick and the type of people who own computers are the type of people who are most likely to own shares.

Day trading will continue to be a minority occupation, for the very good reason that it has a high failure rate. It's rather like those medieval Christian cults that refused to have sex and were thus doomed to die out. At certain points in the cycle, when share prices are racing ahead, it will briefly become popular. But when the market is falling or flat, people will give up.

Interest in the stock market will not die away completely but there will inevitably be disillusionment if, as I predict, returns will be lower in the next twenty years than they have in the past twenty. If the average person earns 7 per cent from equities, lots will earn less than that – particularly those who trade too much, or chase market fads. They will switch their attention elsewhere, perhaps to property or fine wine or classic cars or whatever opportunity seems plausible at the time.

Some investors have already become disillusioned. 'I was greedy and foolish to think I could do better than the professionals. When my shares were in profit, it was too easy, it was like money for free,' says Mark Eccleston, whose investments are down by around 70 per cent. 'I didn't think dotcoms would go belly up, working in London, maybe I got the wrong idea because everyone I knew was buying over the internet.'

This posting on an internet bulletin board probably speaks for many others: 'I expect that I am very far from being alone in holding a portfolio that is worth 40 per cent less than I paid for it. I notice, for example, that many of the unit trusts are 30 per cent down over the last six months. The private investor has been stitched up time without number over the last six months.'[3]

Those who quietly save every month or invest their annual ISA allowance will stick with the market. There are lots of baby boomers who need to save for retirement and are aware that the state will not provide them with a bumper income in their old age. They may, however, have to save more than they currently expect, if they are going to achieve the comfortable lifestyle they crave.

And they may have to be more sensible about their choice of ISA. The most popular funds in March 2000 were based on technology. That was not a wise move. As of 1 December 2000, Aberdeen European Technology had fallen 56.1 per cent over the previous nine months, CCS Global Technology 35.9 per cent, CF Technology Growth 36.4 per cent, Framlington Net Net 59.7 per cent, Henderson Global Technology 31.9 per cent, Jupiter Global Technology 43.3 per cent, M&G Global Technology 25.5 per cent, Premier Technology 49.7 per cent, Rathbone Technology 47.5 per cent, Smith & Williamson Global Technology 54.8 per cent and Société Générale Technology 35.7 per cent.

Share ownership is likely to remain a predominantly middle-class activity. 'Most people who should own shares in the UK already do,' says Jeremy King of ProShare. 'A third of the adult population have no savings at all. Of the two-thirds that do, half have savings of less than £3,500. For the 12 million that have shares, it's about encouraging the building of portfolios.'

A dull market will not be a very exciting business prospect for those who hoped to sell their services to the 'empowered' investors. There will be a winnowing out of the financial websites and of the financial TV channels.

Of course, there will be other fads like dotcom stocks in future. 'The markets are always looking for the next greatest thing,' says Lucy Marcus of Marcus Venture Consulting. 'Even professionals do so because they want to make a lot of money.'

With luck, readers of this book will be both forewarned and forearmed. They will realise that stocks can be driven up to insane levels on flimsy evidence. Share prices are not always an accurate reflection of companies' prospects because many companies' prospects are extremely uncertain.

George Colony of Forrester Research said that 'When we were all in university, we read about the rationality of markets and in fact I think what we've proven is the irrationality – the human spirits which can drive people to invest in some very, very shaky stories.'[4] If markets are not paragons of wisdom, this means they can occasionally be wrong. It also means that there are occasions when governments and other regulators will be forced to step in and correct the excesses of the market – much as that might disturb the purists.

Private investors must learn that buying shares on the basis of tips and vague hunches is a recipe for disaster. 'You've got to understand the business you're investing in. If you don't, then when things go wrong, you won't spot them,' says Jeremy King.

'What we're now left with is the residue,' says Richard Hunter of NatWest Stockbrokers. 'We're not quite at the US stage where every taxi driver talks about the stock market. But stocks and shares are in the public consciousness. What we haven't achieved yet is the education part, teaching people about risk and return.'

'People need to learn about investment planning and portfolio structures, but those things sound deeply tedious. There is nothing wrong with investing in smaller companies as part of your strategy, but it shouldn't be your only strategy,' says Justin Urquhart Stewart of Barclays Stockbrokers.

Work

The current shakeout in the dotcom industry will mean that workers will be reminded of the benefits of security. They will become suspicious of job offers from companies they have never heard of – they will once again want to be sure that the company will still be around in five years' time. The 'creative chaos' of the internet industry will seem less attractive when workers are not sure whether their next pay cheque will arrive. And long working hours are even less appealing if there is no big pay-off at the end.

In a dull stock market, share options will not be the lucrative benefit they used to be. Workers will start to look for more concrete benefits. Executives will seek to re-price failing option schemes – and at some point, institutional investors will rebel at this clear transfer of wealth. Some companies will be forced into introducing schemes in which managers are rewarded for meeting financial targets (cashflow, gross margin, earnings per share etc.) instead of being rewarded for a rising share price, which they may or may not have influenced.

The net

The internet is not going to go away. But perhaps it won't grow quite as quickly as initial enthusiasm expected. It's that dreadful sin of extrapolation again. A survey by PriceWaterhouseCoopers, the accountancy group, found that in 2000, 44 per cent of the US population used the net, a modest increase from the 43 per cent seen in 1999. And those who did use the net spent less time each week – 4.2 hours, compared with 5.3 hours in 1999 and 4.8 hours in 1998.

In the UK, we are further behind the US in adopting the net, so there is still scope for considerable growth. But it wouldn't be surprising if eventually the same trend occurred here. The internet will be rapidly adopted by certain groups of people – the young, the middle classes, the gadget enthusiasts. But there are plenty of things to do in life apart from surfing the net. It is useful to be able to send messages to friends or to work contacts; it is useful to be able to so some shopping over the net.

It is also useful to be able to look up information through the internet. But it is not that exciting. The net makes a great encyclopaedia, but how much of the day do most people want to spend looking through an encyclopaedia? The entertainment currently available does not match that available from the television or from cinema. Eventually, the internet will take its place in the home as one more potential source of entertainment, alongside the TV, radio, hi-fi and games console. And, of course, talking to real people, face-to-face.

It is assumed, particularly by the government, that access to the internet is a universal good which should be extended to all social classes. But some people may just not be interested. Sally Wyatt of the Virtual Society, a group devoted to the social science of electronic technologies, says that 'the possibility of voluntary non-access to the internet is rarely acknowledged'. She cites a US study dating from 1996, which showed that 11 per cent of those surveyed had stopped using the internet, with cost and loss of interest among the reasons cited.[5]

In business terms, there will be a change in attitude. The internet will become just one more tool of business rather than a class of business by itself. All large businesses will use it, just as all businesses use the telephone. But now that the bubble has burst, small companies may take their time about switching to a net-based model. 'You're finding that a lot of the periperhal companies – the ones who had been hyped into thinking that they had to take action – have now lost interest,' says David Bowen of Net Profit.

Already people are saying that the main beneficiaries of the internet will be old economy companies – those consumer companies with established brand names who can use it as another distribution system and those industrial companies who can use it to cut costs. People will increasingly use the net for shopping for certain goods (B2C), those that are sufficiently standardised not to need a physical inspection. 'Once they wire the whole country, and people everywhere have unmetered access, B2C will come round again,' predicts Lucy Marcus of Marcus Venture Consulting.

Some dotcom companies will survive – AOL has just about assured itself of doing so by its merger with Time Warner. Amazon.com has its doubters – it certainly continues to lose a ton of money – but in terms of customer service, it (literally) delivers the goods and it has established a brand name. It will surely survive, although perhaps not as the all-things-to-all-men retailer it has been aiming to be. At the time of writing, Lastminute has lots of cash left and the name has resonance. I wouldn't be very confident of its independent survival, but someone might well be tempted to buy the business.

And the industry is still in its infancy. There will be many more developments and, perhaps, dotcom giants that have yet to be born. 'The fundamental uses of the internet are very difficult to understand. It is going to change the way that business and the world operate in lots of quite subtle ways. Businesses have to think quite hard about how they can take advantage,' says David Bowen.

Culture

Television is a world of fads and fashions. Quiz shows have been popular before, but eventually the format becomes rather dull. Ratings for the US version of *Who Wants to Be a Millionaire?* have already started to slip, now that so many people have achieved the feat. In a desperate attempt for ratings, formats will become progressively more extreme with contestants having to take greater risk and face greater humiliations in order to earn the prize. The format of the *Weakest Link* is but one step along the road, but eventually it will lead to diminishing returns.

Gambling will substantially increase, now it is open to so many in easy formats like the internet and interactive television. Inevitably there will be stories of families ruined by a combination of the remote control and the racing from Sandown. Inevitably there will be scandals as unscrupulous betting companies, trading from obscure parts of the world, prey on the vulnerable. There will be hand-wringing documentaries about the problem on television and a call for greater regulation. But restricting the internet will prove impossible.

And that probably goes for many of the changes that we have seen in the book. There will undoubtedly be a public reaction against the easy money culture at some point, but limiting the ability of people to trade, gamble, or earn vast sums will prove impossible. Alas, pious lectures from governments or journalists will probably prove ineffective in persuading people that big money rarely comes easily; hard experience is a much better teacher. We will all have to learn how to handle the risks.

References

Barber, Brad M. and Odean, Terrance, 'Boys Will Be Boys: Gender, Overconfidence and Common Stock Investment', Working Paper, University of California in Davis, September 1999, available online at http://www.gsm.ucdavis.edu/~bmbarber/research/default.html.
—— 'Online Investors: Do the Slow Die First?', Working Paper, University of California in Davis, October 2000, available online at http://www.gsm.ucdavis.edu/~bmbarber/research/default.html.
—— 'Too Many Cooks Spoil the Profits', *Financial Analysts Journal*, January 2000.
Black, F. and Scholes, M., 'The Pricing of Options and Corporate Liabilities', *Journal of Political Economy*, May–June 1973.
Black, Peter, *Mirror in the Corner: People's Television*, Quality Book Club, 1973.
de la Vega, Joseph, *Confusion de Confusiones*, 1688; republished as a volume together with *Extraordinary Popular Delusions and the Madness of Crowds* by Charles Mackay, John Wiley & Sons, 1996.
Diamond, John, 'But That's Another Story', *Evening Standard*, 29 November 2000.
Emshwiler, John, *Scam Dogs and Mo-Mo Mamas: Inside the Wild and Woolly World of Internet Trading*, John Wiley & Sons, 2000.
Goldman Sachs, 'Is the Internet Better than Electricity?', Global Economics Paper 49, privately circulated, July 2000.
—— 'Technology and the New UK Economy: Following in the Footsteps of the United States', privately circulated, December 2000.

Gordon, Robert J., 'Does the New Economy Measure up to the Great Inventions of the Past?', NBER Working Paper W7833, 2000.

Greenwood, Jeremy, *The Third Industrial Revolution: Technology, Productivity and Income Inequality*, AEI Press, 1997.

James, Clive, *The Crystal Bucket: Television Criticism from the Observer 1976–79*, Picador, 1982.

Kadlec, Charles W., *Dow 100,000: Fact or Fiction?*, New York Institute of Finance, 1999.

KPMG Consulting, 'The Economic Value and Public Perceptions of Gambling in the UK', privately circulated, May 2000.

London Business School/Korn Ferry International, 'Tomorrow's Leaders Today: Career Aspirations and Motivations', privately circulated, November 2000.

Mandel, Michael J., *The Coming Internet Depression: Why the High-Tech Boom Will Go Bust, Why the Crash Will Be Worse Than You Think and How to Prosper Afterwards*, Basic Books, 2000.

Martin, Bill, 'Drivers of the New Economy', Phillips & Drew Occasional Paper 10, privately circulated, 12 October 2000.

Morgan Stanley Dean Witter, 'The Technology Growth Cycle', privately circulated, October 2000.

Odean, Terrance, 'Are Investors Reluctant to Realize Their Losses?', *Journal of Finance* 53, 1998.

Oliner, Stephen and Sichel, Daniel, 'The Resurgence of Growth in the Late 1990s: Is Information Technology the Story?', Federal Reserve Board, February 2000.

Parsley, David, 'Internet Workers Want to Swap Share Options for Bigger Salaries', *Sunday Times*, 26 November 2000.

Perkins, Anthony B. and Perkins, Michael C., *The Internet Bubble: Inside the Overvalued World of High-Tech Stocks – And What You Need to Know to Avoid the Coming Shakeout*, HarperCollins, 1999.

Potter, Jeremy, *Independent Television in Britain* [vol. III], Palgrave, 1988.

Raven, James, 'A Wheel of Fickle Fortune', *Independent*, 18 February 1994.

Sendall, Bernard, *Independent Television in Britain*, vol. I, *Origin and Foundation 1946–62*, Palgrave, 1982.

—— *Independent Television in Britain*, vol. II, *Expansion and Change 1958–68*, Palgrave, 1983.

Shiller, Robert J., *Irrational Exuberance*, Princeton University Press, 2000.

Smith, Terry, *Accounting for Growth*, 2nd edn, Random House Business Books, 1996.

Smithers, Andrew and Wright, Stephen, *Valuing Wall Street: Protecting Wealth in Turbulent Markets*, McGraw-Hill, 2000.

Tawney, R. H., *Religion and the Rise of Capitalism*, Penguin, 1990.

Wyatt, Sally, 'They Came, They Surfed, They Went Back to the Beach: Why Some People Stop Using the Internet', paper prepared for the Society for Social Studies of Science conference, San Diego, October 1999.

Notes

Introduction

1 If houses are included, the proportion of national wealth owned by the top 10 per cent increased from 50 to 52 per cent over the same period.

2 Brad M. Barber and Terrance Odean, 'Boys Will Be Boys: Gender, Overconfidence and Common Stock Investment', Working Paper, University of California in Davis, September 1999, available online at http://www. gsm.ucdavis.edu/~bmbarber/ research/default.html.

3 Arguably, it wasn't really free. Investors had previously been mutual owners of the building societies and insurance companies. But the issue of shares gave them the chance to cash in on their ownership.

Chapter 1 – Trading Places

1 *Barron's*, 4 December 2000.

2 Some of that decline was offset by the growth of unit trust ownership. Unit trusts, a collective savings vehicle for private investors, grew from owning 0.5 per cent of the market in 1957 to 6.7 per cent in 1997.

3 Brad M. Barber and Terrance Odean, 'Online Investors: Do the Slow Die First?', Working Paper, University of California in Davis, October 2000, available online at http://www.gsm.ucdavis.edu/bmbarber/research/default.html.

4 Via e-mail.

5 Durlacher shares rose 12,000 per cent between the start of 1999 and

the spring of 2000. At the time of writing, they had subsequently dropped by 90 per cent.

6 He e-mailed me in May 2000.

7 Terrance Odean, 'Are Investors Reluctant to Realize Their Losses?', *Journal of Finance* 53, 1998.

8 Interviewed in early December 2000.

9 Barber and Odean, 'Online Investors'.

10 Brad M. Barber and Terrance Odean, 'Too Many Cooks Spoil the Profits', *Financial Analysts Journal*, January 2000.

11 The savings ratio tends to be high during recessions, when people are cautious about the future, and low during booms, when they feel confident. Why save for a rainy day when the sun is perpetually shining?

12 Goldman Sachs, 'Technology and the New UK Economy Following in the Footsteps of the United States', privately circulated, December 2000.

13 This is simply another version of the dividend yield/dividend growth calculation.

14 Andrew Smithers and Stephen Wright, *Valuing Wall Street: Protecting Wealth in Turbulent Markets*, McGraw-Hill, 2000.

15 The authors make no specific forecasts about the UK market but it is safe to say that, if Wall Street falls by 60 per cent, the FTSE 100 will be dragged down with it.

16 Robert Shiller, *Irrational Exuberance*, Princeton University Press, 2000.

17 Charles W. Kadlec, *Dow 100,000: Fact or Fiction?*, New York Institute of Finance, 1999.

18 It's actually not as wild as it sounds. For a start, the Dow rose from 1,000 in 1982 to 10,000 in 1999, exactly the same proportionate increase. The Dow would only have to rise by around 11 per cent a year to meet his target.

Chapter 2 – Tipping Point

1 A continuous tape with the latest share prices would be sent through to brokers' offices. This 'ticker tape' was also used as a form of confetti to shower on winning sports teams and war heroes – hence the term a 'ticker tape parade'.

2 Those who agree to buy and sell shares on a continuous basis in a wide range of shares. A marketmaker can be an individual or the firm he or she works for.

3 In early 2001, the first-mentioned was trading at 9p, the second at 0.75p and the third at 2.25p from a high of 22.75p. The website can be found at http://www.iii.co.uk/insider.

4 John Emshwiler, *Scam Dogs and Mo-Mo Mamas: Inside the Wild and Woolly World of Internet Trading*, John Wiley, 2000.

5 The academic tide has swung against efficient market theory, as shown by several of the studies cited in this book. Behavioural finance studies the irrationality of investors. But knowing that investors are irrational doesn't make it any easier to beat the index. How long will the irrationality last? And what form will it take?

6 Issued 10 May 2000 and available online at the Commission's website http://www.pcc.org.uk.

7 For anyone interested, I own shares in Pearson, the parent company of the *Financial Times*. Apart from that, I confine myself to unit and investment trusts. Because I had savings accounts with various building societies, I did acquire shares in the likes of the Halifax when they demutualised. I have since sold them.

Chapter 3 — The Net

1 Interviewed on the BBC Radio 4 programme *In Business*, 11 May 2000.

2 Interview with the author.

3 Interviewed in the BBC Radio 4 programme *In Business*, 11 May 2000.

4 Ibid.

5 Quoted in *The Economist*, 18 November 2000.

6 Interviewed for the BBC Radio 4 programme *In Business*, 6 July 2000.

7 This hardly seems surprising. The company was essentially assembling a sophisticated mailing list. In most houses, unsolicited mail from financial services companies goes straight in the bin.

8 See Chapter 2 for an explanation of this versatile breed.

9 Goldman Sachs, 'Is the Internet Better than Electricity?', Global Economics Paper 49, privately circulated, July 2000.

10 Robert J. Gordon, 'Does the New Economy Measure up to the Great Inventions of the Past?', NBER Working Paper W7833, 2000.

11 Stephen Oliner and Daniel Sichel, 'The Resurgence of Growth in the Late 1990s: Is Information Technology the Story?', Federal Reserve Board, February 2000. I am grateful to James Barty of Deutsche Bank for drawing my attention to this work.

12 Jeremy Greenwood, *The Third Industrial Revolution: Technology, Productivity and Income Inequality*, AEI Press, 1997. Again thanks to James Barty of Deutsche Bank for an explanation of Greenwood's work.

13 Morgan Stanley Dean Witter, 'The Technology Growth Cycle', privately circulated, October 2000.

14 Privately circulated.

15 Michael Mandel, *The Coming Internet Depression: Why the High-Tech Boom Will Go Bust, Why the Crash Will Be Worse Than You Think and How to Prosper Afterwards*, Basic Books, 2000.

Chapter 4 – Putting a Price on Shares

1 Everyone wants to buy shares that are good value.

2 Bill Martin, 'Drivers of the New Economy', Phillips & Drew Occasional Paper 10, privately circulated, 12 October 2000.

3 The average for the late 1990s was 10 per cent a year; the forty-year average was 7 per cent. By relative prices, Martin means that the change in prices of IT goods is x per cent below that of the general price level.

4 'The Technology Growth Cycle'.

5 Quoted in *Barron's*, 20 November 2000.

6 Price–earnings ratios can either be historic, which means they are based on published profit figures, or prospective, which means they are based on forecast results. Bulls tend to focus on prospective ratios, particularly for growth stocks, since it makes the shares look cheaper (since the ratio is lower). Bears tend to point out that forecasts are often wrong; the historic ratio is more reliable.

7 FTSE and other index providers are in the process of changing these rules. As of 2001, companies' weight in the FTSE indices will depend on the 'free float' – the proportion of publicly tradable shares. That will significantly reduce the captive demand for some companies' shares.

8 Anthony B. Perkins and Michael C. Perkins, *The Internet Bubble:*

Inside the Overvalued World of High-Tech Stocks – and What you Need to Know to Avoid the Coming Shakeout, HarperCollins, 1999.

9 The company's share price rose so fast that it had a bonus issue to reduce it. This didn't affect the value of the overall company but made the shares look 'cheaper'. See Chapter 2 on this illusion.

10 Terry Smith, *Accounting for Growth*, 2nd edn, Random House Business Books, 1996. Mr Smith now works for the broker Collins Stewart.

Chapter 5 – Career Options

1 They were following a very successful precedent. Bill Gates dropped out of Harvard to found Microsoft.

2 London Business School/Korn Ferry International, 'Tomorrow's Leaders Today: Career Aspirations and Motivations', privately circulated, November 2000.

3 He was interviewed in October 2000.

4 The FTSE All-Share index, the broadest measure of the UK market, fell in 2000 for the first time since 1994.

5 F. Black and M. Scholes, 'The Pricing of Options and Corporate Liabilities', *Journal of Political Economy*, May–June 1973.

6 Reported in David Parsley, 'Internet Workers Want to Swap Share Options for Bigger Salaries', *Sunday Times*, 26 November 2000.

Chapter 6 – Taking a Punt

1 I should declare an interest. I am an old friend of Angus.

2 Interviewed by the author for the *FT* in the autumn of 1999.

3 Interviewed by the author for the *FT* in the autumn of 1999.

4 IG Index is an exception to this rule. It will not hedge all its exposure but will leave itself exposed a small amount either way. Although this means it loses money on two or three days out of twenty, Stuart Wheeler believes over the longer term the effect is to enhance profits because the firm saves on hedging costs.

Chapter 7 – A Cultural Shift

1 James Raven, 'A Wheel of Fickle Fortune', *Independent*, 18 February 1994.

2 *Independent Television in Britain*, 3 vols., Polgrave, 1982–8.

3 Peter Black, *Mirror in the Corner: People's Television*, Quality Book Club, 1973.

4 1 April 1979, reprinted in Clive James, *The Crystal Bucket: Television Criticism from the Observer 1976–79*, Picador, 1982.

5 KPMG Consulting, 'The Economic Value and Public Perceptions of Gambling in the UK', privately circulated, May 2000.

6 Shiller, *Irrational Exuberance.*

7 John Diamond, 'But That's Another Story', *Evening Standard*, 29 November 2000.

8 The man who backed them at Creation Records, Alan McGee, had just floated his new company, Poptones, on the market.

9 This is a typical problem with tax-based savings schemes. When John Major introduced the TESSA (Tax Exempt Special Savings Scheme) for cash deposits, lots of people simply transferred their money from a taxable building society account to a tax-free account. Little new money was saved as a result.

Conclusion

1 A name strikingly close to *merde*, the French word for shit.

2 R. H. Tawney, *Religion and the Rise of Capitalism*, Penguin, 1990.

3 Author Greyfox 1 on the Interactive Investor bulletin board (http://www.iii.co.uk/insider).

4 Interviewed for the BBC Radio 4 programme *In Business*, 6 July 2000.

5 Sally Wyatt, 'They Came, They Surfed, They Went Back to the Beach: Why Some People Stop Using the Internet', paper prepared for the Society for Social Studies of Science conference, San Diego, October 1999.